ARCH301
STUDIO MUECKE

COD | DOA | FALL 2016

I0102692

P-1

Hog Press
922 5th Street
Ames, IA 50010
USA

www.hogpress.com
editor@hogpress.com

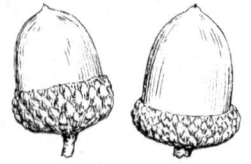

HOG PRESS

P1: PROJECT 1, ARCH301 STUDIO MUECKE | CoD | DoA | FALL 2016

Copyright © 2016 by Megan Dunham, Zach Hansen, Evan Harrison, Ayla Hendrickson, Miranda Herpfer, Nathaniel Jones, Bassam Kaddoura, Jeff Klynsma, Michael McKinney, Vanessa Miller, Carlos Poémape, Atalie Ruhnke, Yang Zheng, and Yihuan Zhang.

All rights reserved.

For our Instagram page, go to www.instagram.com/arch301muecke/

No part of this book may be reproduced in any form by any electronic or mechanized means (including photocopying, recording, or information storage and retrieval) without written permission, except in the case of brief quotations embodied in critical articles and reviews.

For more information, please visit www.hogpress.com

ISBN-10:   0-9848942-2-5

ISBN-13:   978-0-9848942-2-2

Cover design and interior layout © 2016 by polytekton

Overview

This book consists of work by fourteen students in the Arch 301 Architectural Design III third-year studio of the Bachelor of Architecture program at Iowa State University. Mikesch Muecke is the instructor and the students are Megan Dunham, Zach Hansen, Evan Harrison, Ayla Hendrickson, Miranda Herpfer, Nathaniel Jones, Bassam Kaddoura, Jeff Klynsma, Michael McKinney, Vanessa Miller, Carlos Poémape, Atalie Ruhnke, Yang Zheng, and Yihuan Zhang

Project 1 Description

Observatory

Individual Work. Consider the design of an observatory for a site in Brookside Park. What the observatory allows you to observe has to involve physical/sensory stimuli. To get started read pages 1-37 of Juhani Pallasmaa's The Eyes of the Skin (on Blackboard) and research the work of James Turrell, especially his sky catchers and the ongoing work in the Roden Crater project.

Parameters

1. Location

The site for the observatory has to be located within the following boundaries of Brookside Park: southside edge of 13th Street, westside edge of Brookridge Avenue, southside edge of southern Union Pacific rail line, eastside edge of tree line running along western side of the baseball fields and the forest south of 13th Street.

2. Elevation

There has to be an elevation difference of at least 12 vertical feet between the different levels of the observatory ground plane (the building cannot be on a flat piece of ground).

3. Apertures

The building has to have apertures in the horizontal planes to bring light in and allow views out.

4. Above + Below

Half of the volume of the building has be below ground, the other half above. You need to employ both stereotomic and tectonic modes of creating space.

5. Size

The conditioned space should not be more than 300 feet square. The unconditioned space can be no more than twice the space of the conditioned space.

Final Review Requirements for Wednesday, 28 September, 2016

1. ¼"-1' model of design in the site
2. Sections (at least two) at ¼"=1'
3. Plans at 1/8"=1'
4. Site plan
5. Hybrid drawing showing preessistenze ambientali in section perspective
6. Diagrams: circulation, program, structure, wind, sun, etc.
7. 150 words describing the project: "My idea for the design is...."

Table of Contents

Project 1

Sensory Observatory

Megan Dunham

Reparian

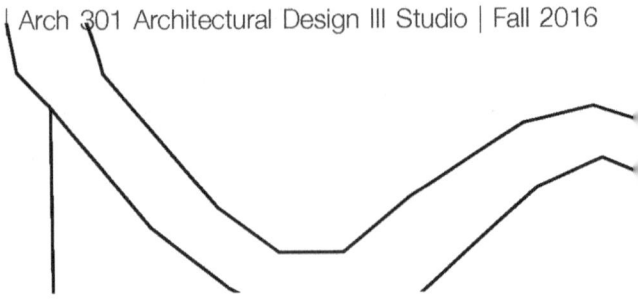

Adam Cvijanovic

Starting off with inspiration from our Artist we were tasked to create an abstract visual of collage of the site, Brookside Park, Ames, Iowa. From here we created both an abstract site model and site plan. After our field trip, I was inspired to change my design. From here I created a space for observing the river. On one side you may relax and enjoy the view, the other potential to play in the river, and above you can observe a 180 degree view of the river. This space allows you to have a closer experience with the river.

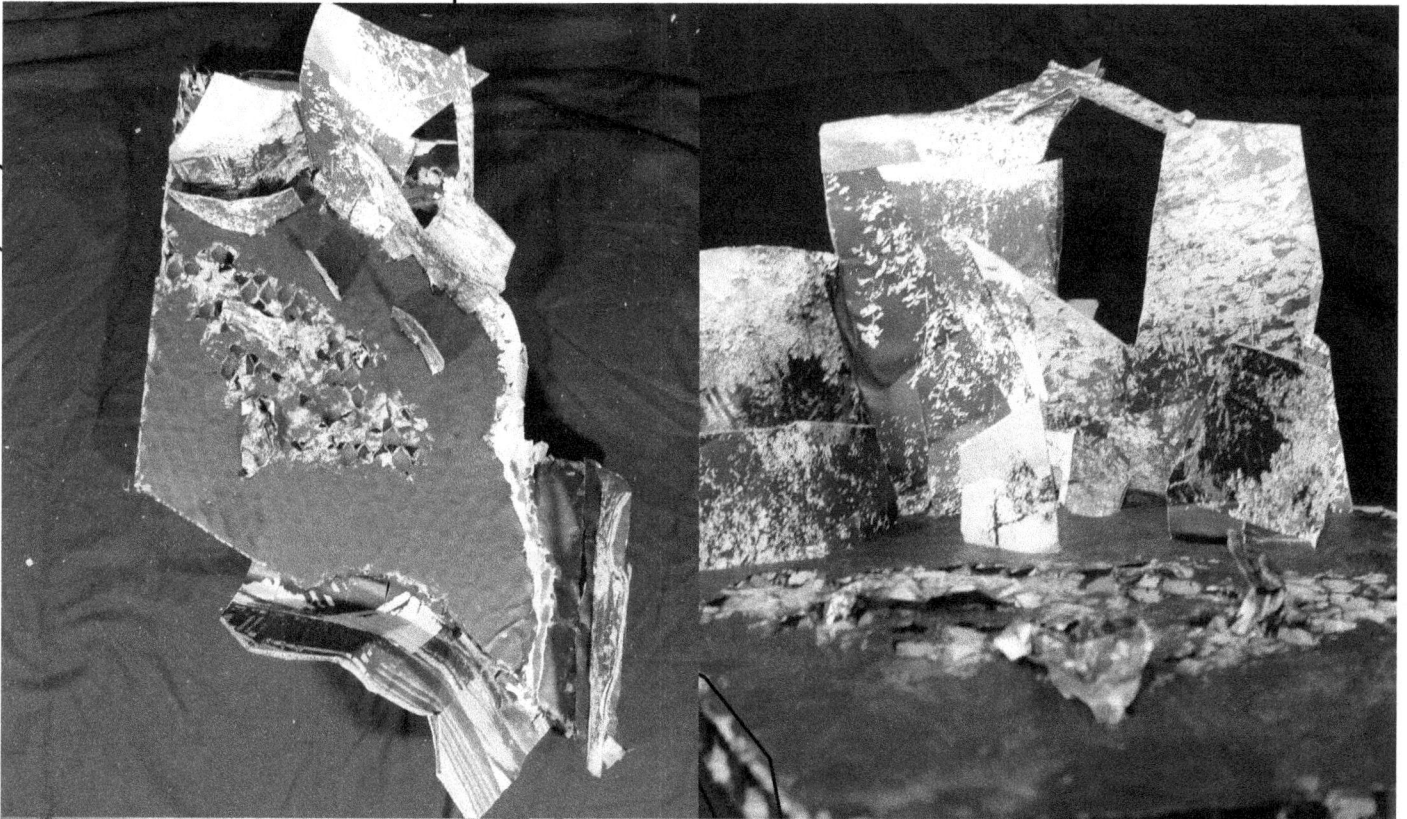

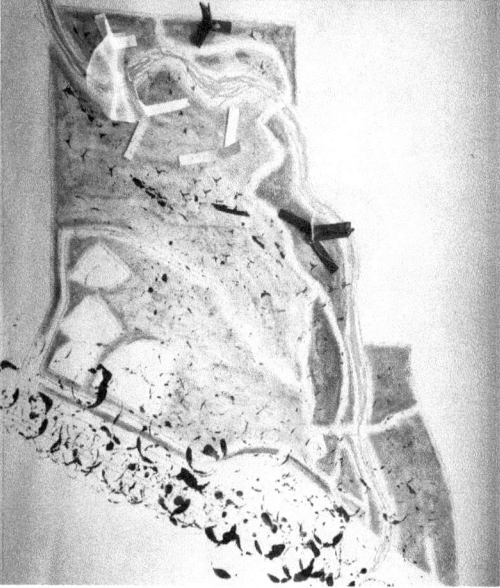

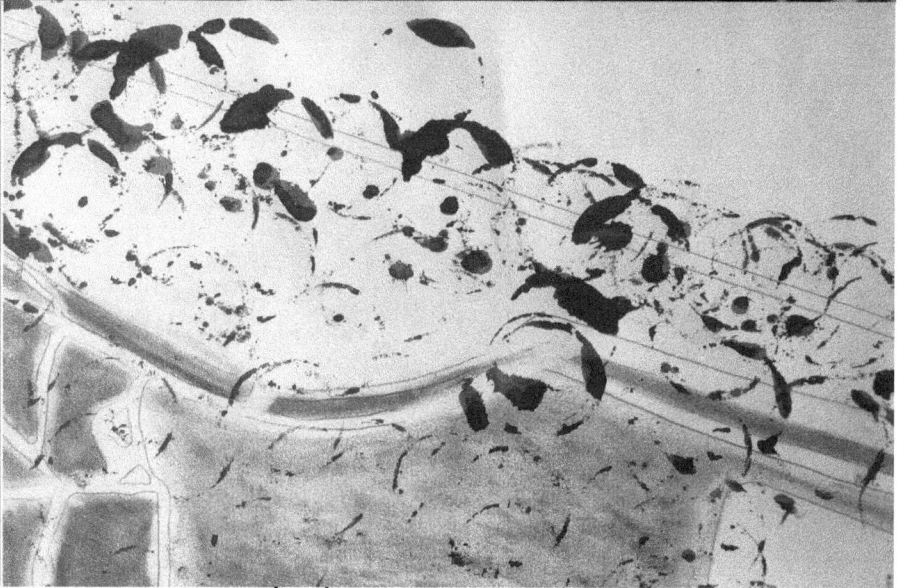

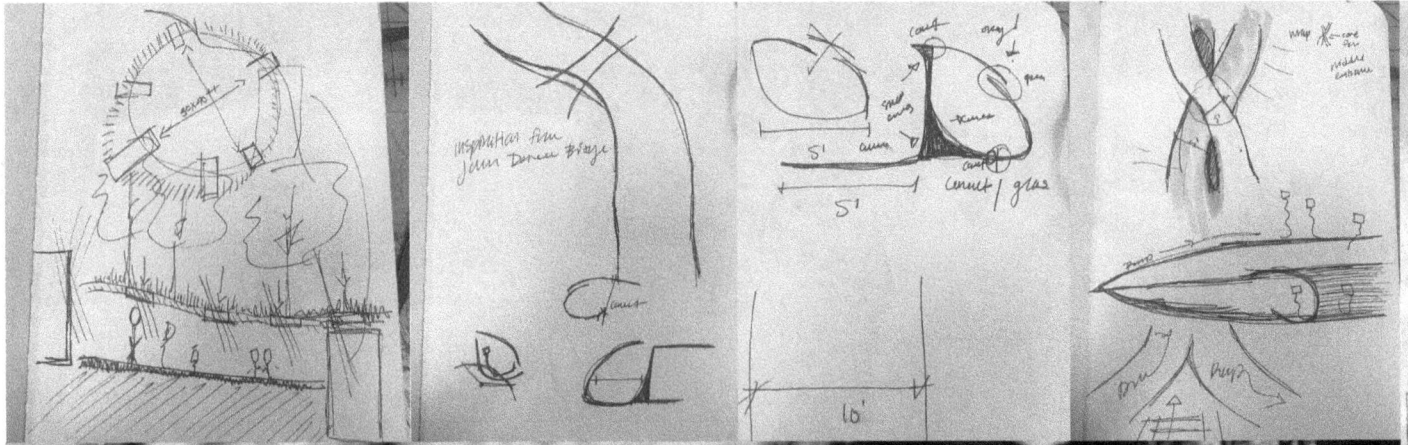

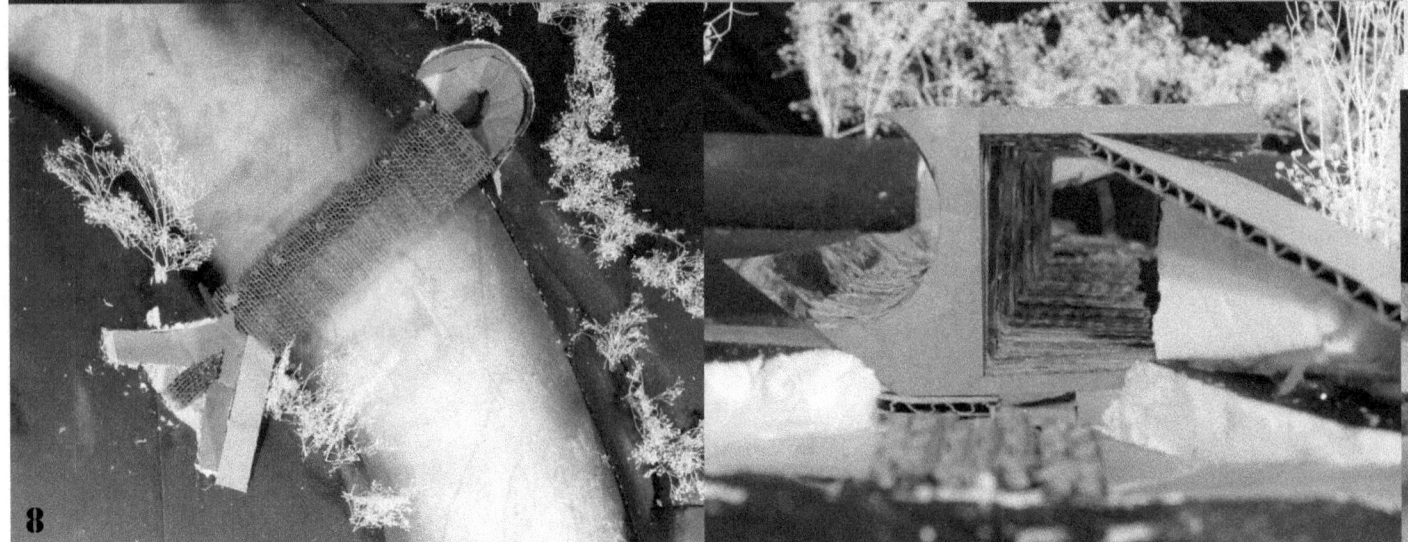

The Riparian

Brookside Park, Ames IA

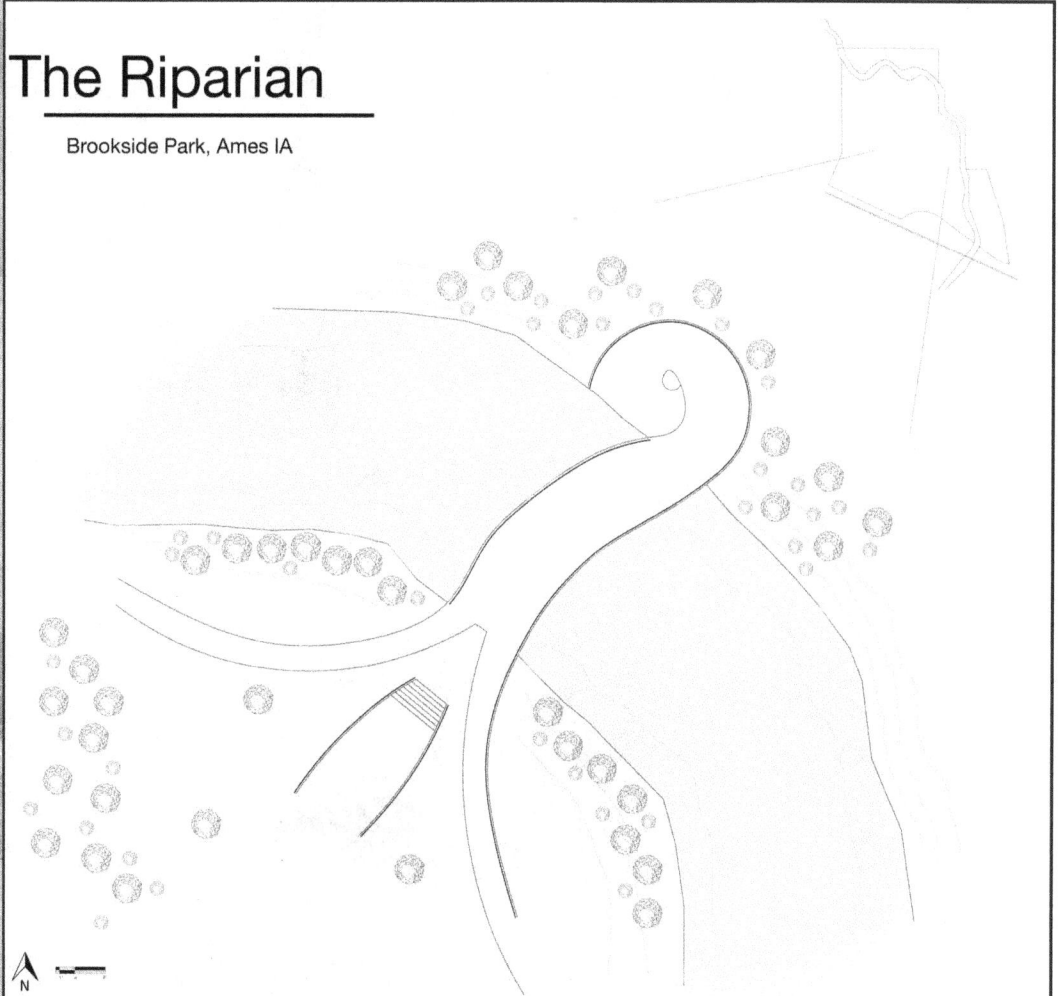

N

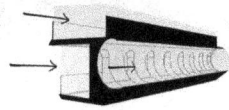

Circulation >

Assembly >

Rain >

< River Flow

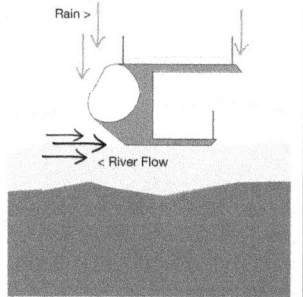

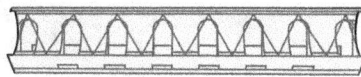

Possible Structure >

< Weather

Project 1

Sensory Observatory

Zachary M. Hansen

Star Catcher

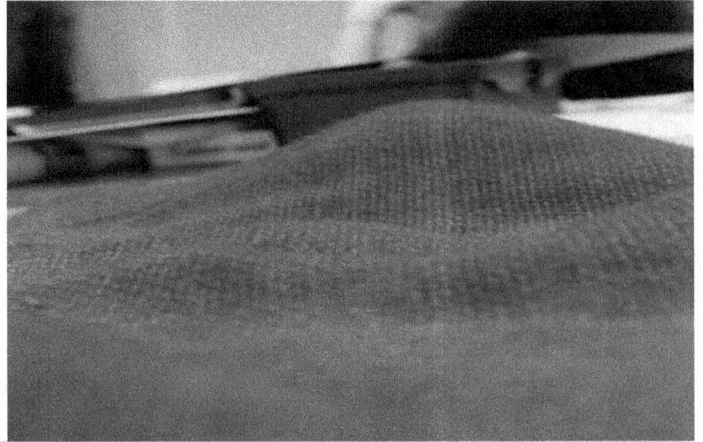

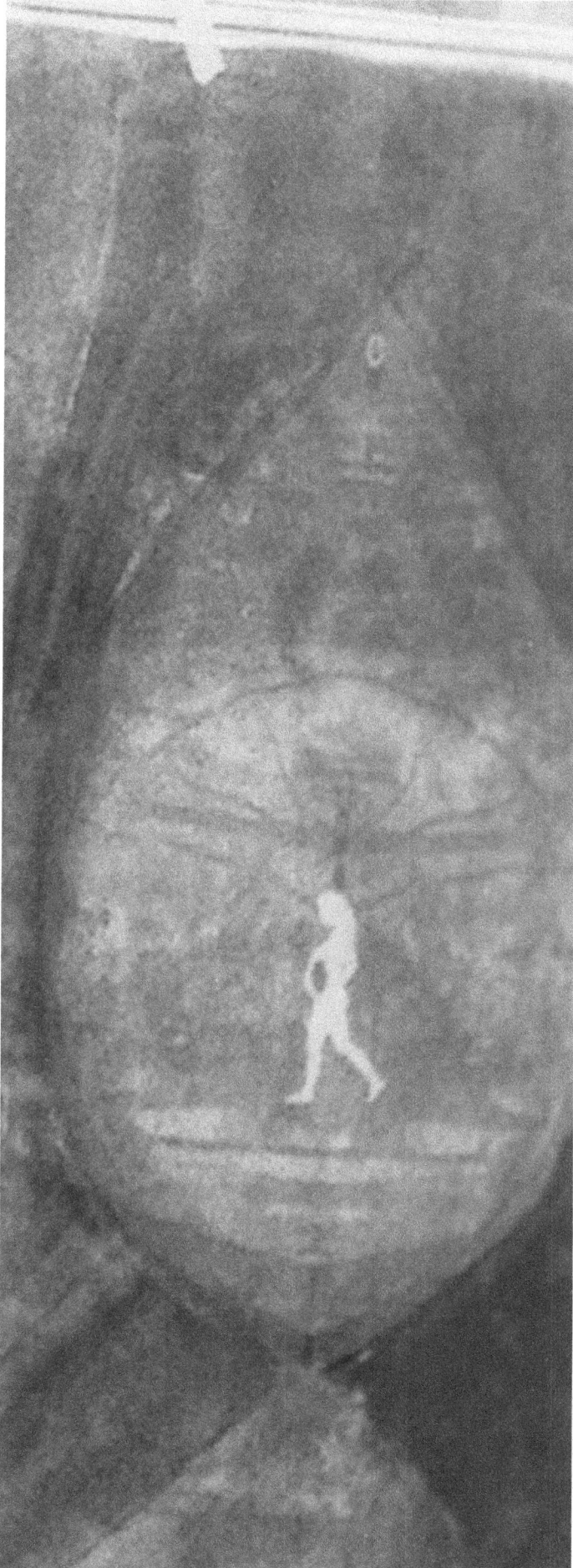

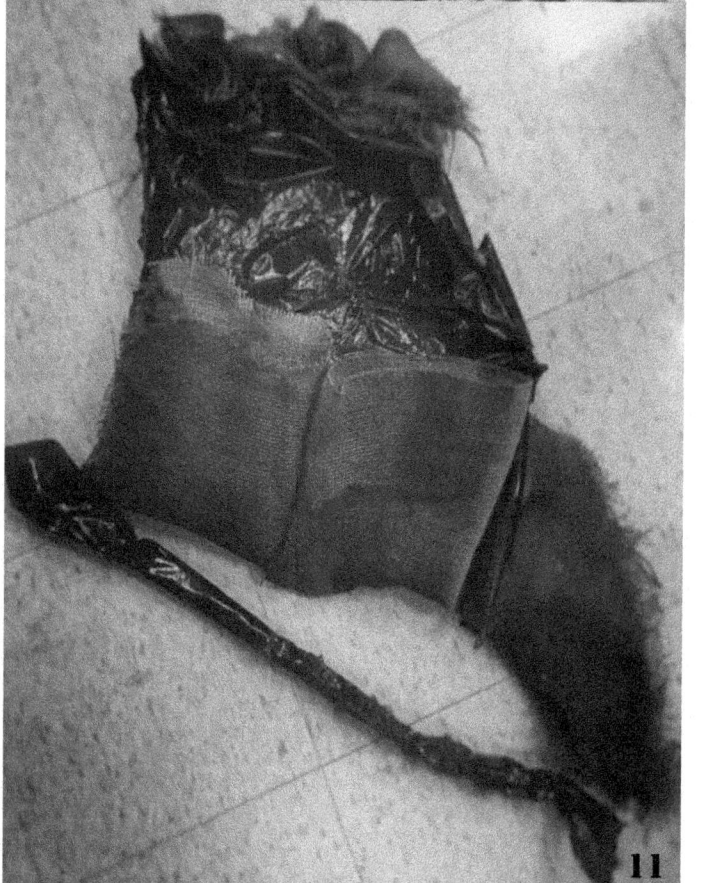

"The idea behind the design of this building is to bring to the people and the people to the sky. Too often it is how do people interact with the building, but here, in t observatory, I am attempting to have the building inter the people instead. The building blocks the occupant' senses on the lower level and immerses them in all of senses on the upper level. The shape of the building in people within it to look upwards to view the stars on e level. It also creates a star scape on both the upper lev providing a view out, and on the lower level by punch in the ceiling to allow light to pour into the lower level create a new galaxy of sorts. The Star Catcher Observ brings the stars to the earth and the earth to the stars.

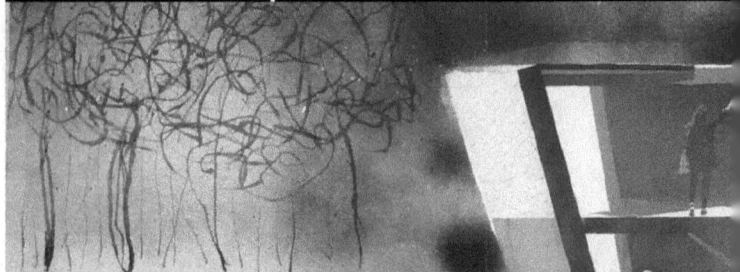

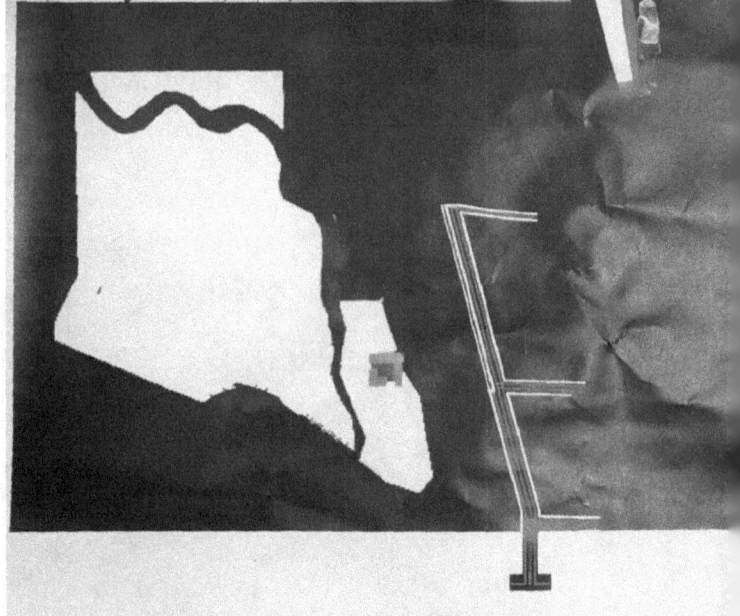

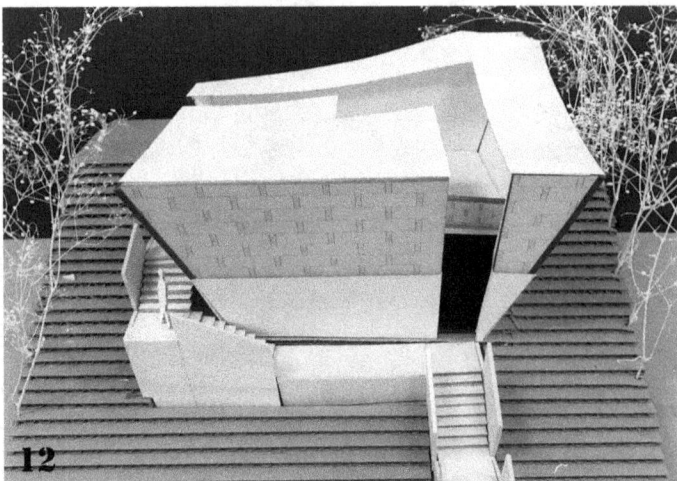

June 21

Sept. 21
Mar. 21

Dec. 21

Project 1

Sensory Observatory
Evan Harrison
Zion Pavilion

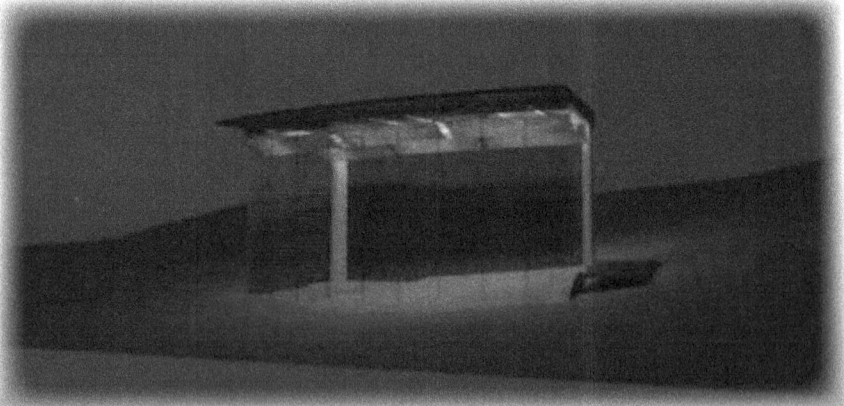

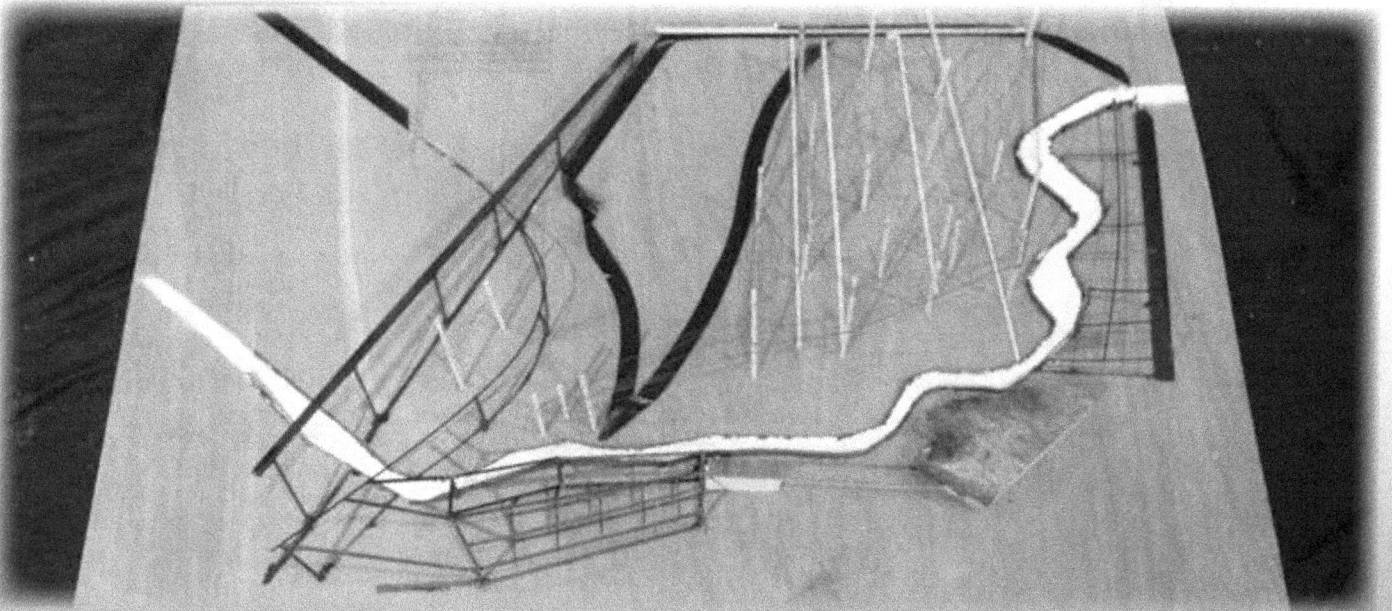

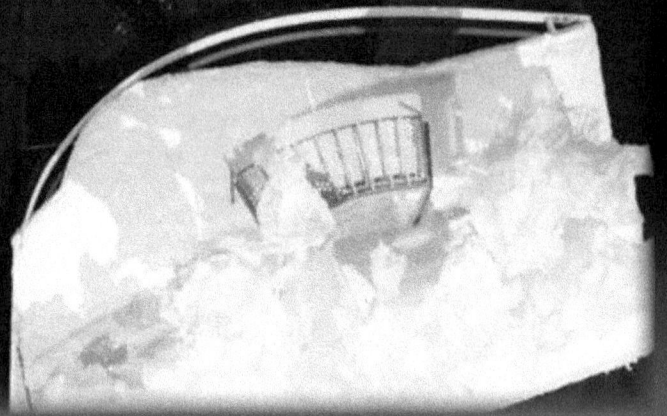

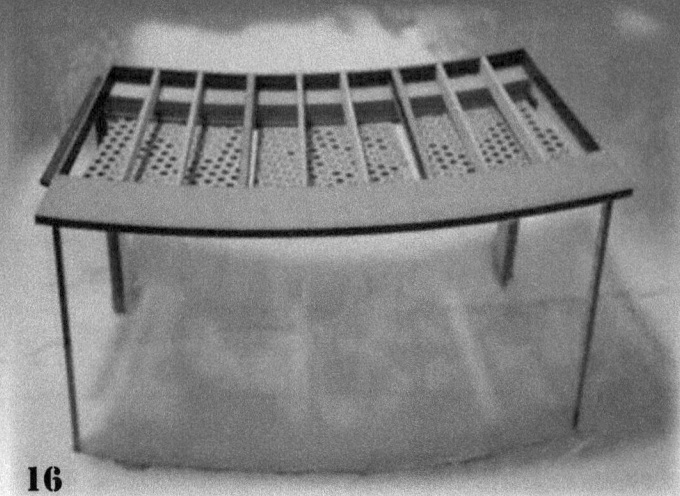

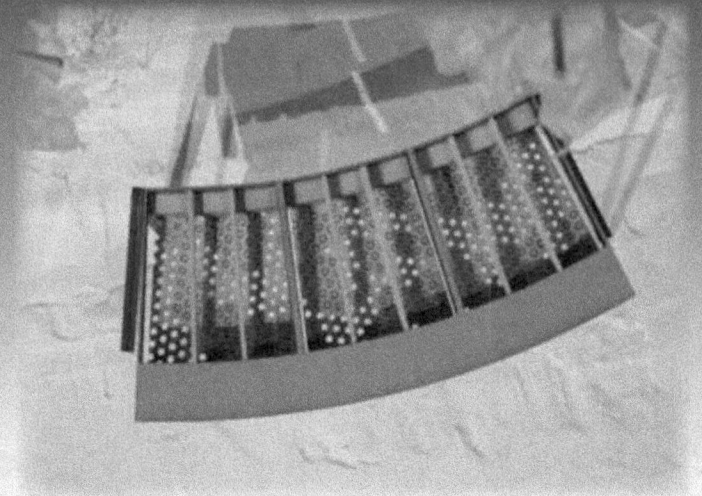

16

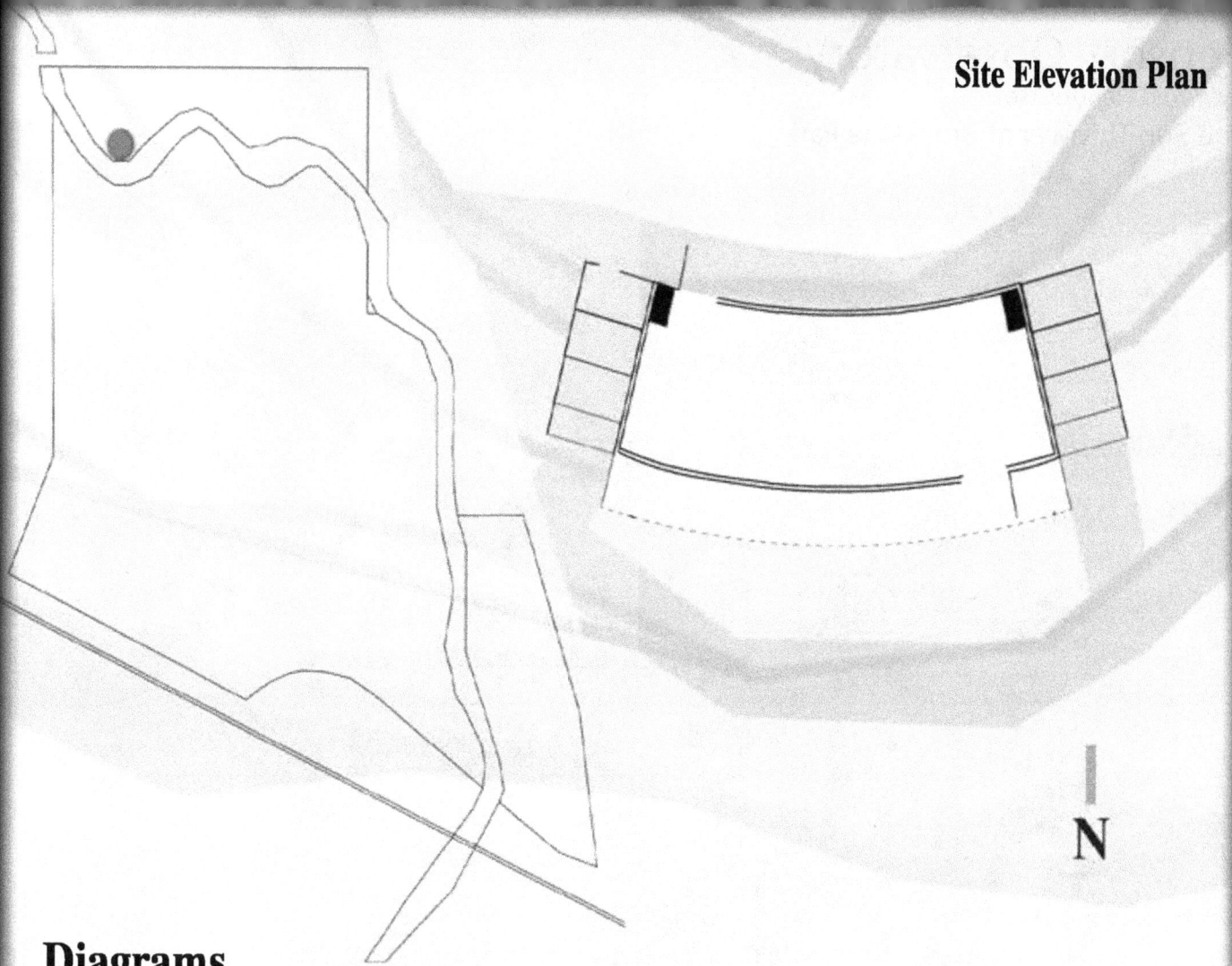

N

Diagrams

Low   Medium   High

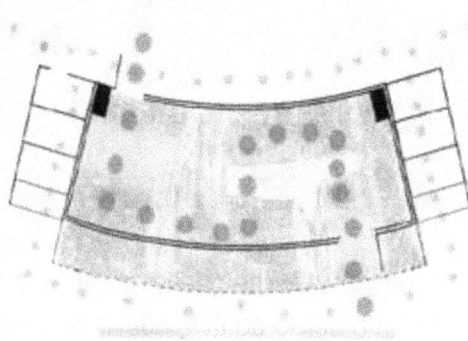

Circulation Analysis

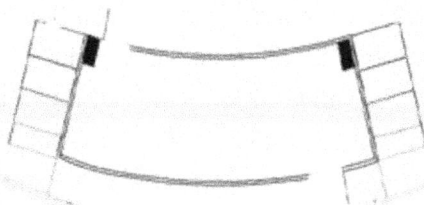

Sun Diagram

Sensory Observatory

Ayla Wild Hendrickson

The Sun Thrower at Brookside Park

I approached this project with the goal of creating a monolithic, accessible structure that appeared to readily change with seasons. In order to do this, I devised a two-tiered concrete observatory, with a main wall that curved with the path of the sun on the summer solstice. The upper level would be plated with an orange, stainless steel mosaic that would reflect sunlight differently depending on the time of day and the time of year. During the summer, the orange would contrast with the green of the trees, and in the winter inspire a sense of warmth in the user. The mosaic was inspired by the abstract artist Ellsworth Kelly, who's paintings often consisted of only two or three colors that served as an extreme distillation of a nature scene. By placing the structure on the bank of the creek, the upper level of the observatory provides views down river. The lower level of the observatory, accessible by stairs as well as a ramp, provides a more haptic experience by allowing users to interact with the water. As the structure has no glass or mechanical systems, it can safely flood when the creek rises. Evidence of past floods will show in the patina of the concrete.

Section B to B'

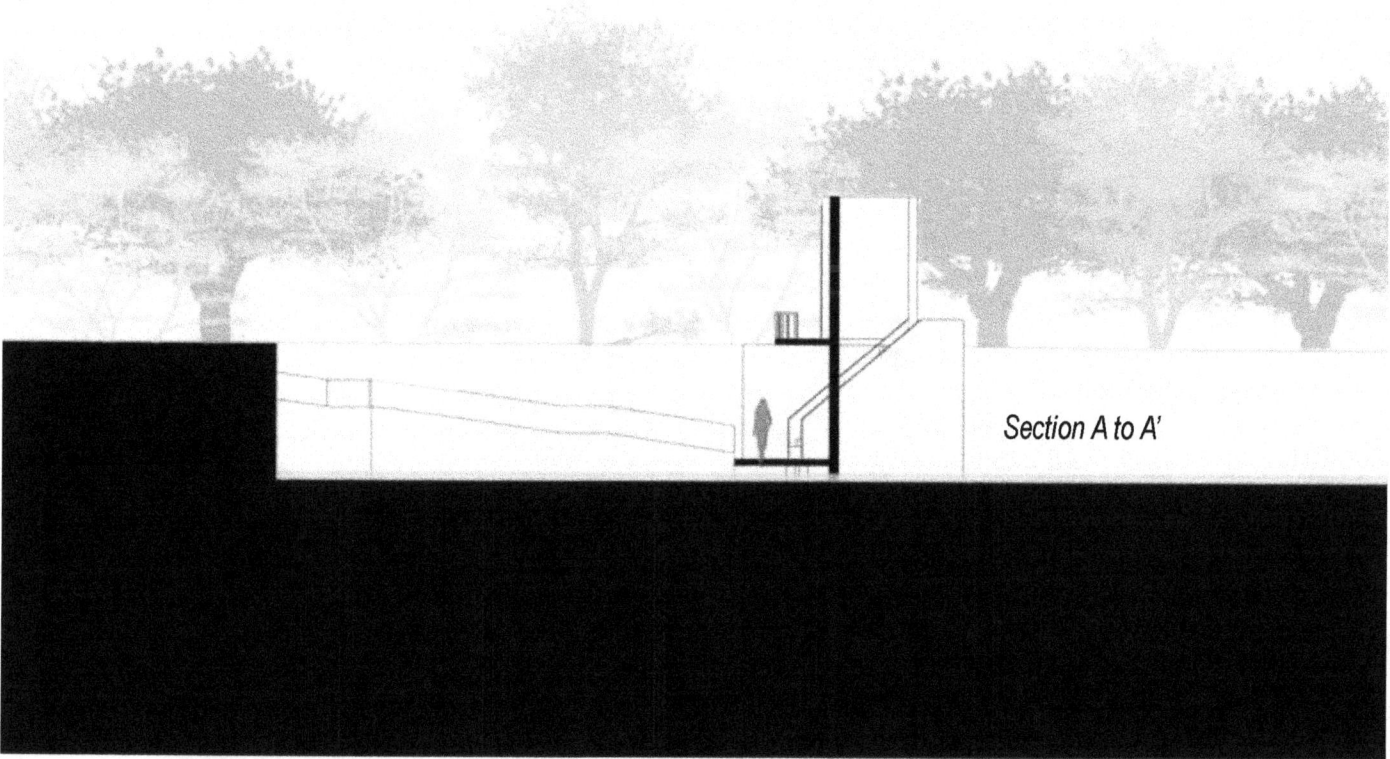

Section A to A'

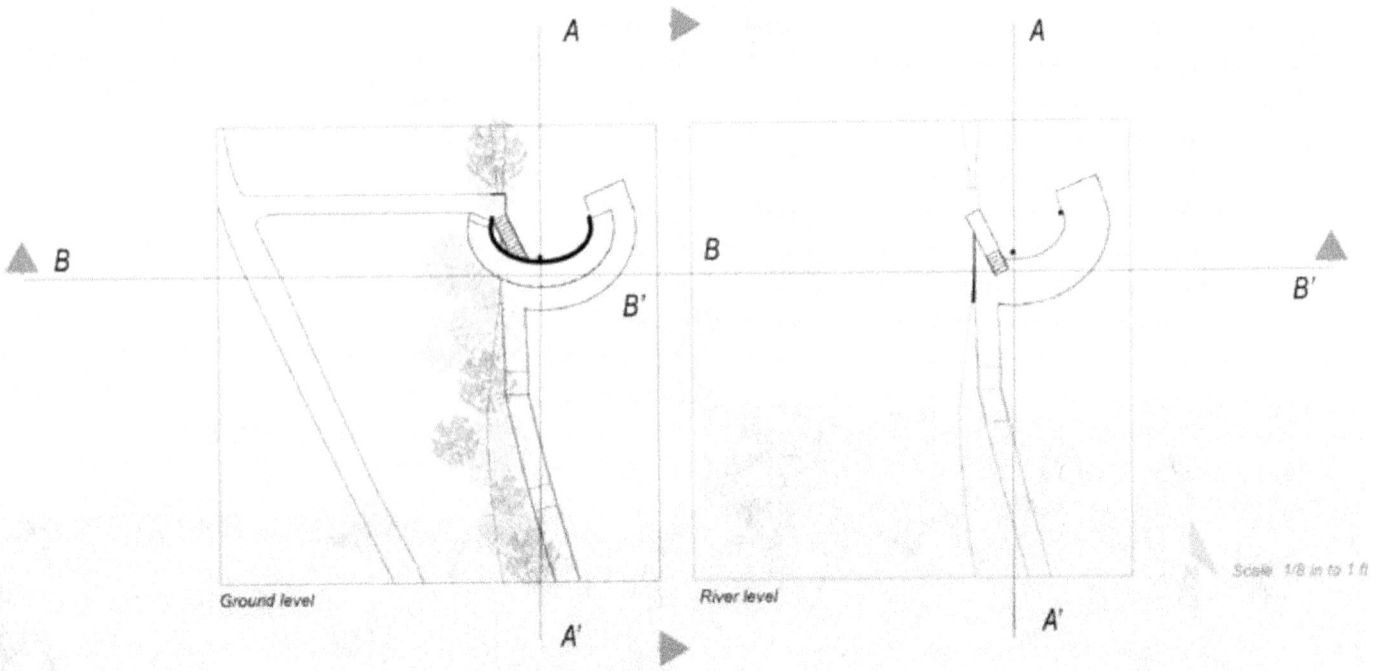

Ground level

River level

Scale 1/8 in to 1 ft

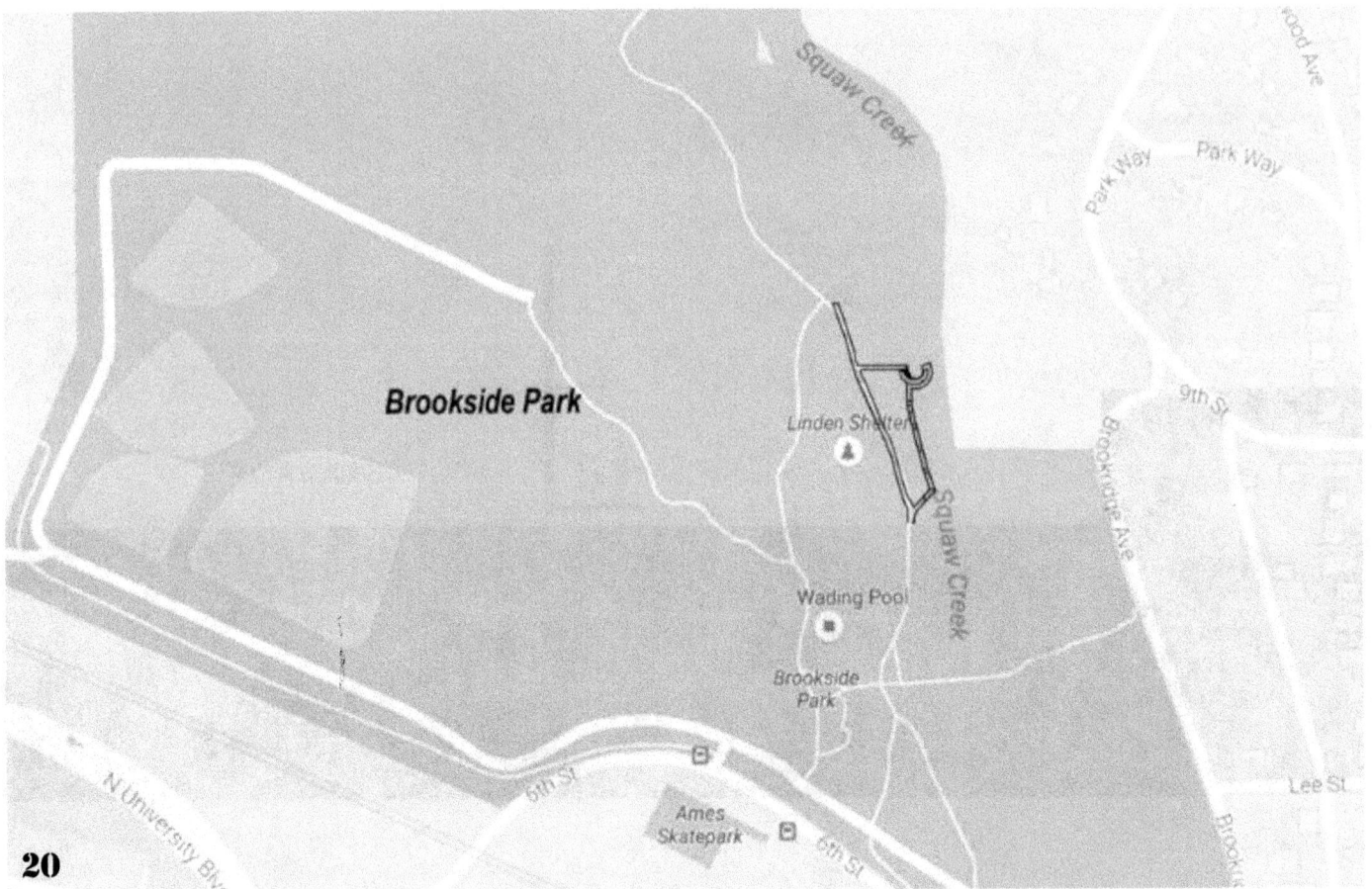

Brookside Park

Linden Shelter

Wading Pool

Brookside Park

Squaw Creek

Ames Skatepark

Process/ Iterations

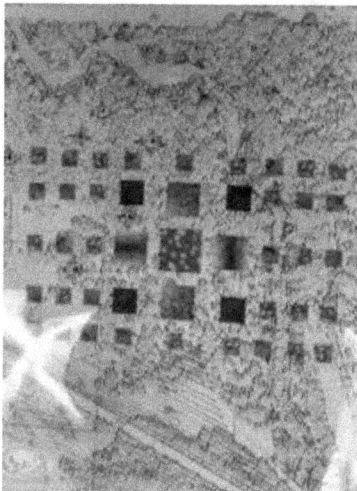

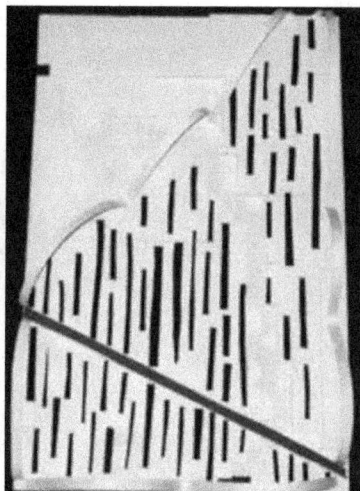

Project 1

Sensory Observatory

Miranda Herpfer

Passageway

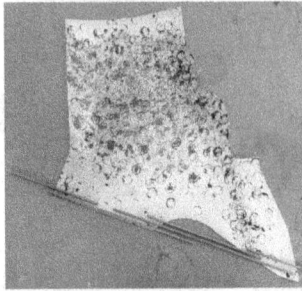

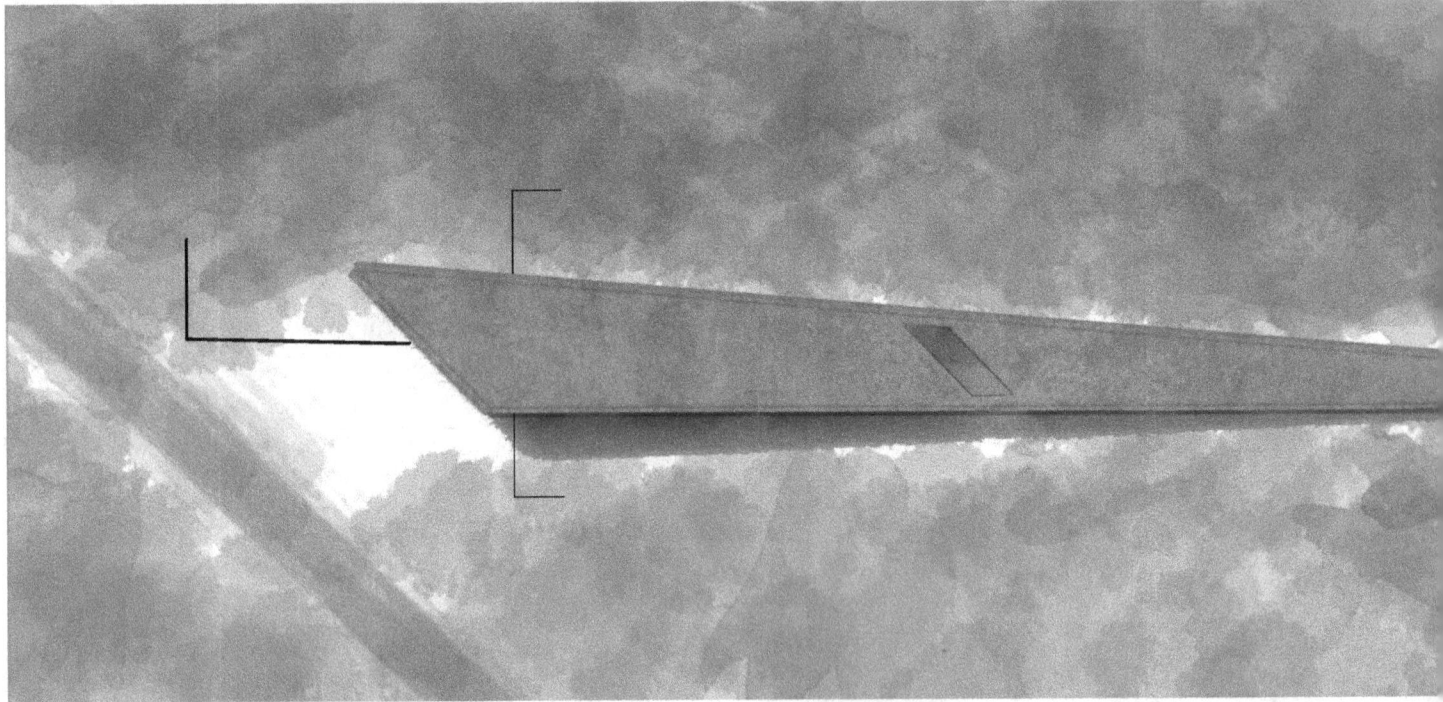

LARGE APERATURE

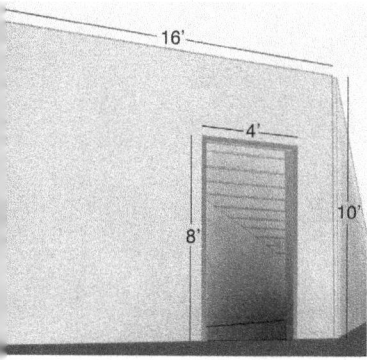

MEDIUM APERATURE

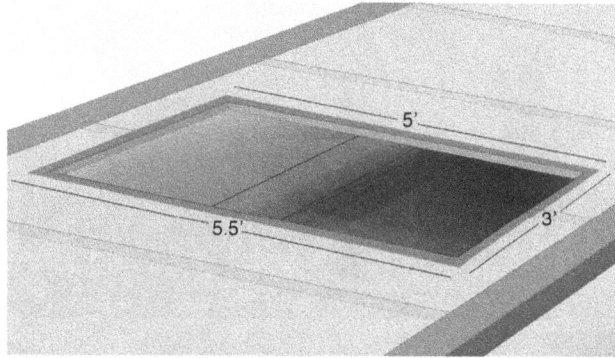

SMALL APERATURE

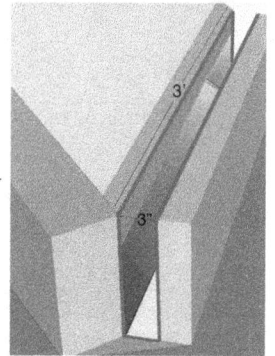

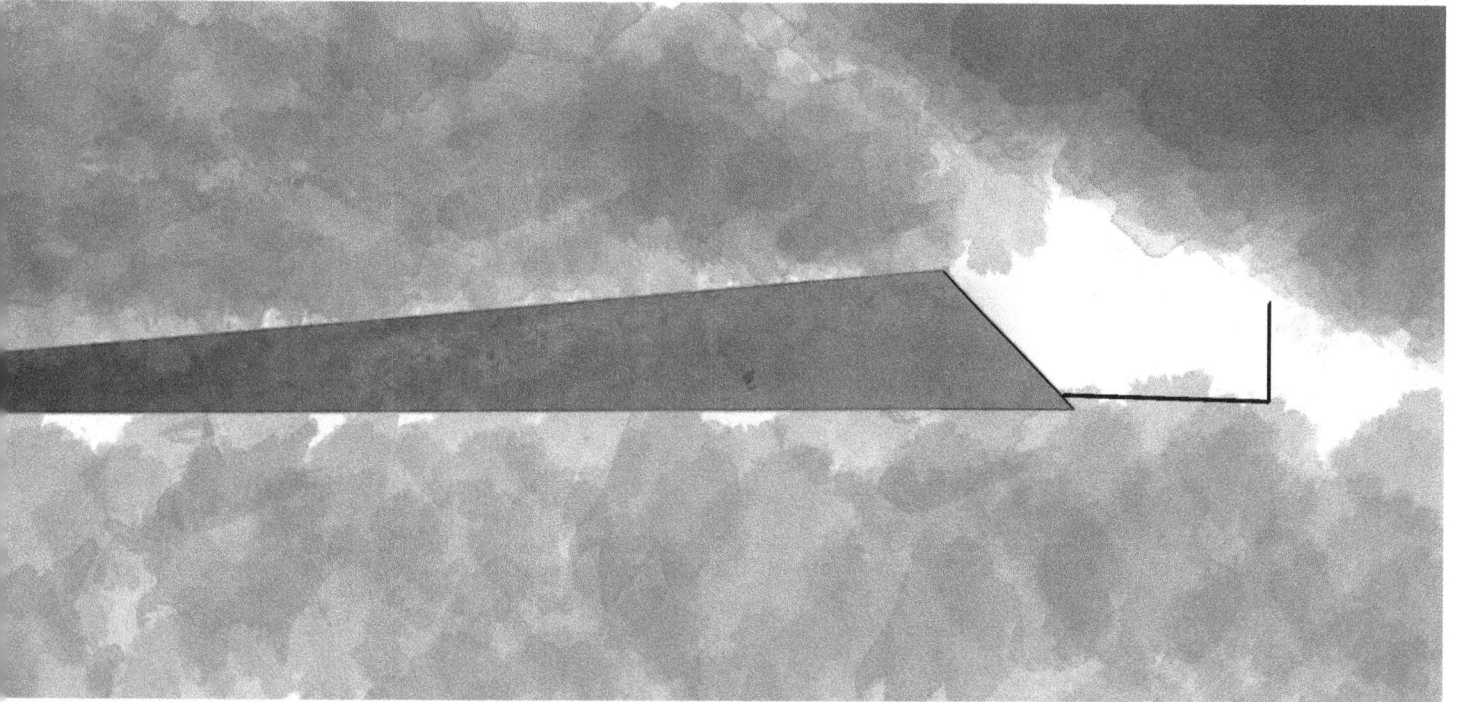

ABOVE

BELOW

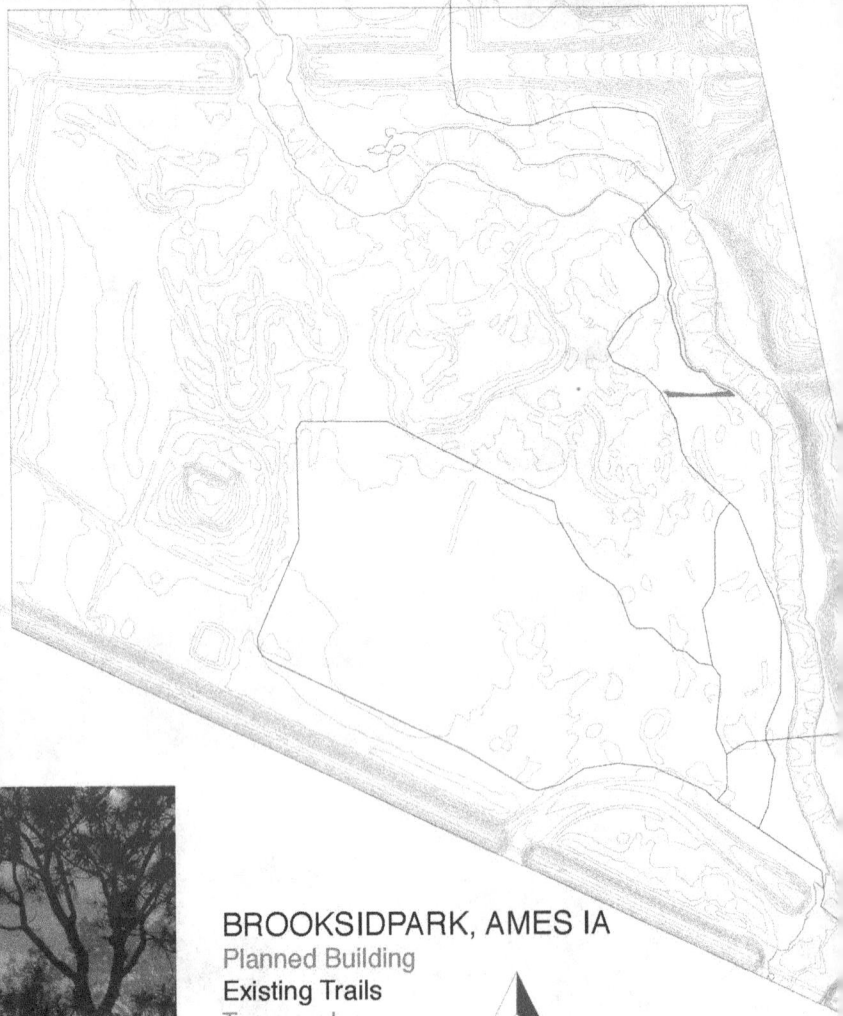

BROOKSIDPARK, AMES IA
Planned Building
Existing Trails
Topography
Train

River

CONDITIONED SPACE

UNCONDITIONED SPACE

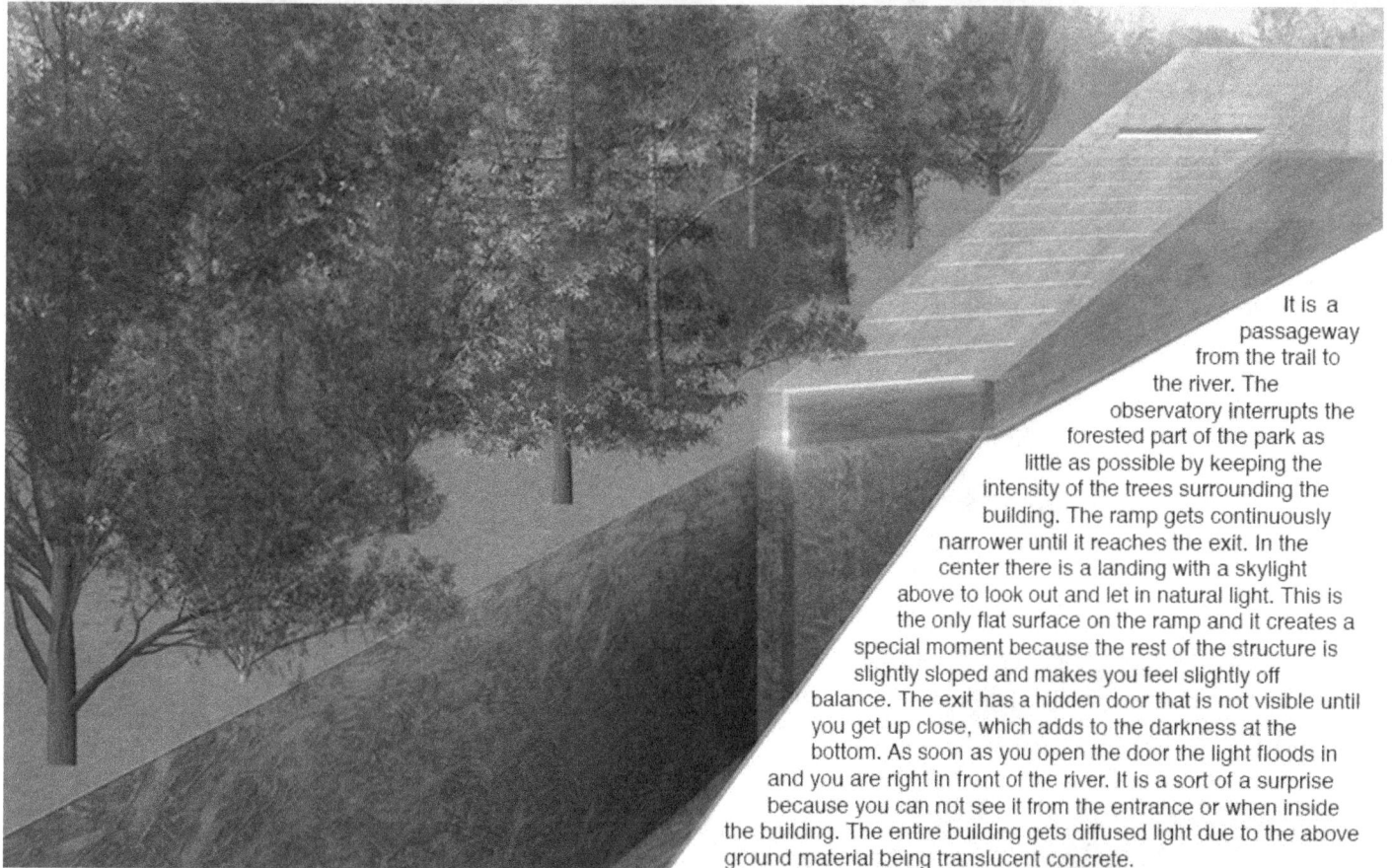

It is a passageway from the trail to the river. The observatory interrupts the forested part of the park as little as possible by keeping the intensity of the trees surrounding the building. The ramp gets continuously narrower until it reaches the exit. In the center there is a landing with a skylight above to look out and let in natural light. This is the only flat surface on the ramp and it creates a special moment because the rest of the structure is slightly sloped and makes you feel slightly off balance. The exit has a hidden door that is not visible until you get up close, which adds to the darkness at the bottom. As soon as you open the door the light floods in and you are right in front of the river. It is a sort of a surprise because you can not see it from the entrance or when inside the building. The entire building gets diffused light due to the above ground material being translucent concrete.

Sensory Observatory

Nathaniel Jones
Ambient Wind

SITE ANALYSIS OF BROOKSIDE PARK

(Top Right)
Visualization of the cycles of the forests using site locations.

(Bottom Left)
Two dimensional site map of the park highlighting the multiple layers of noise.

(Bottom Right)
Three dimensional hard angled site map of forest density using reclaimed wood.

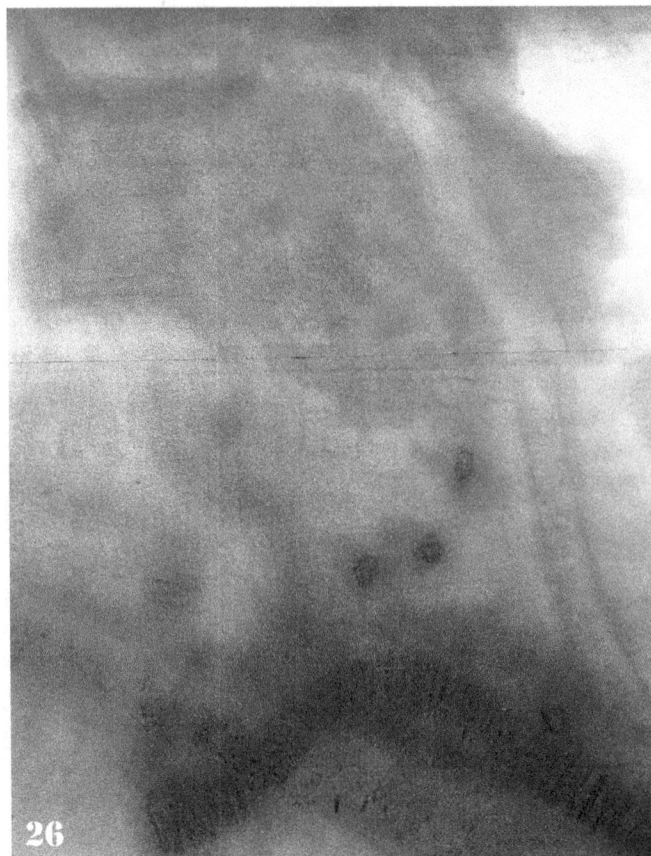

IDEA DEVELOPMENT

Looking at sound sculptures using hallow metal pipes such as "Singing Ringing Tree" along with pan flute instruments the concept of having a structure that amplified the gentle howl and hum of the wind arose. After further development a play of interior and exterior spaces along the hillside of the site was wanted.

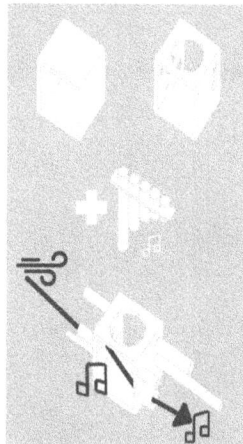

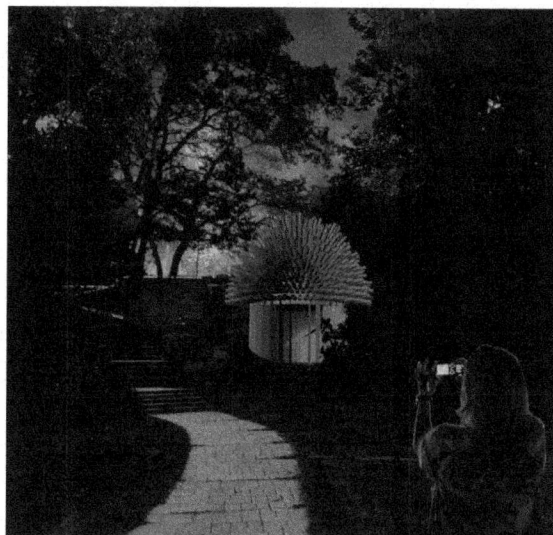

EARLY SELCTION AND ELEVATION

REDEVELOPMENT OF DESIGN USING MODEL

Early design of concept had the wind dome as a parabolic shape with tubes places randomly within and situated up out of the ground on a platform. Thinking that this spacial construction did not relate enough to the hill upon it was situated along with not being a diverse enough of an experience the design moved towards being mostly underground but allowing apertures for light. From this point to final the paces would go farther underground and two small spaces, one with an oculus pointing into the trees of the hill, would be included.

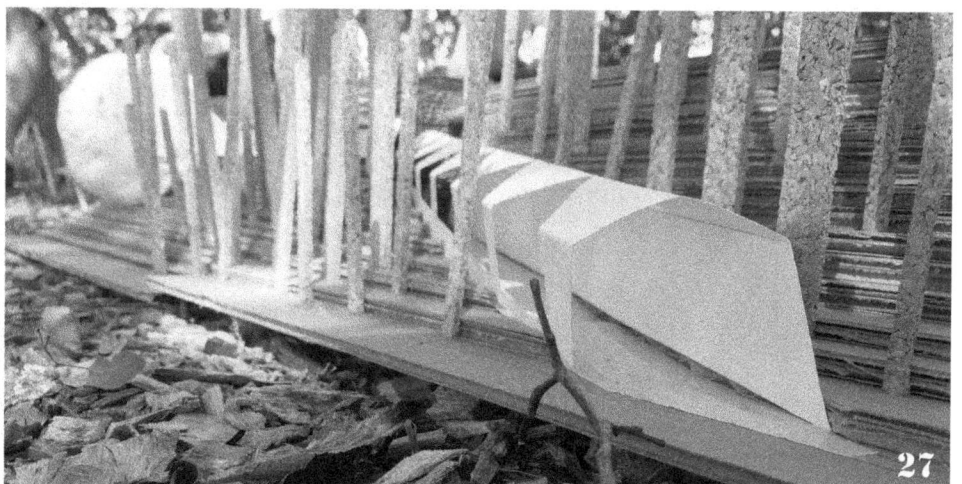

27

FINAL DRAWINGS
Hand drawn in first ever effort to do so for final

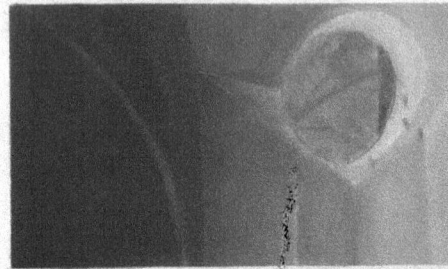

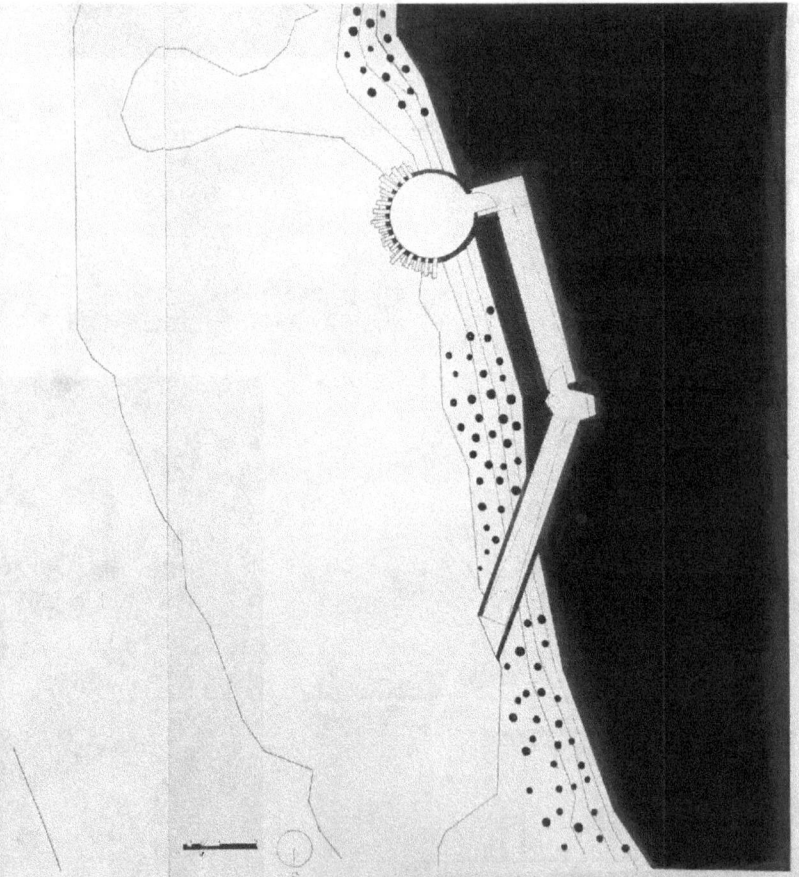

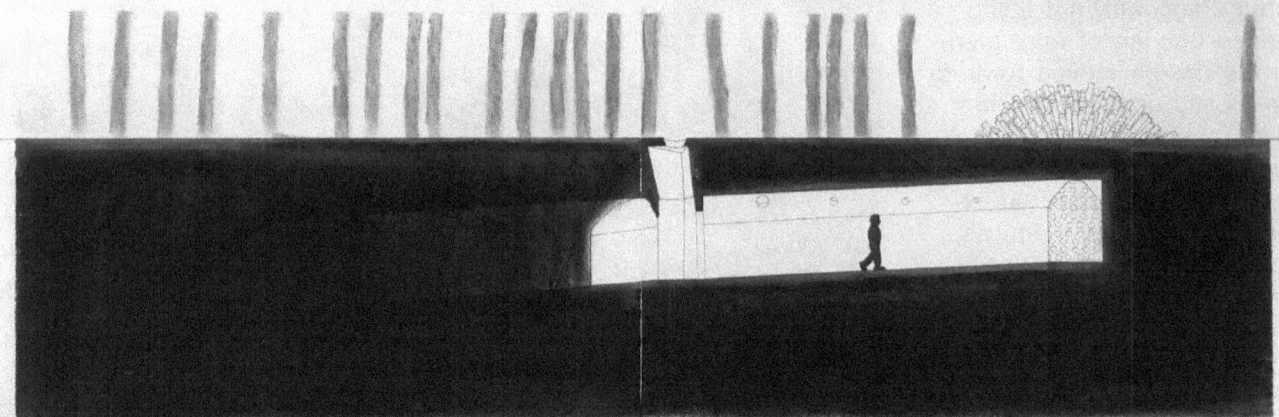

FINAL MODEL

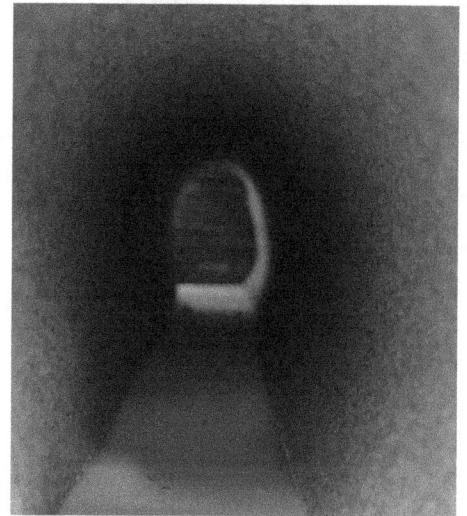

Project 1

Sensory Observatory

Bassam Kaddoura

Osservatorio in Brookside Park

Visualisations of Site and Abstract Maps

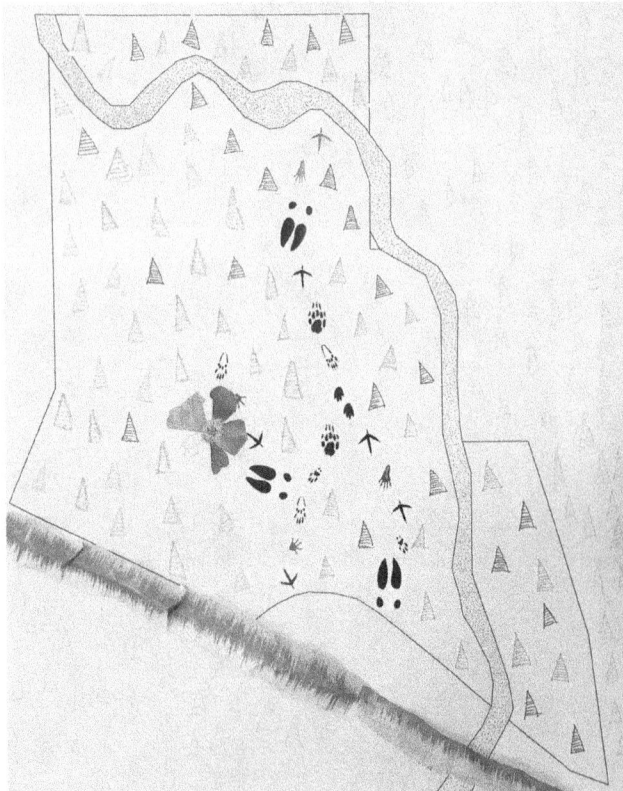

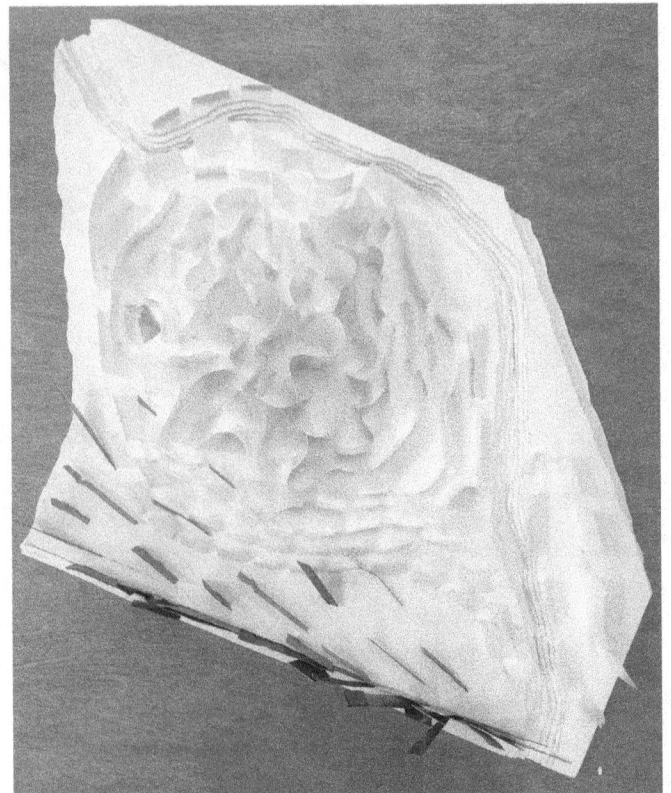

Precedents

Brookside Park brings nature to an urban town, acting as a disengagement and escape from the repetitive grid nature of Ames. Osservatorio is a proposal for an addition to the park which further mystifies and intensifies the park's frequenters and visitors. The walkway to the observatory is not connected to the path, making its find a challenge. Once found, multiple experiences are inherently present in the sequence of Osservatorio. The exterior experience provides a voyeurist encirclement of the central cone, because of the use of translucent concrete. The slits in the tunnel not only create a visual pacing, but also create an auditory experience that is emitted by the surroundings and the wind. Once underground, the extended corten on the top of the cone, reflects the south facing light, creating a differentiation between sky, steel and glass.

First Digital and Physical Model

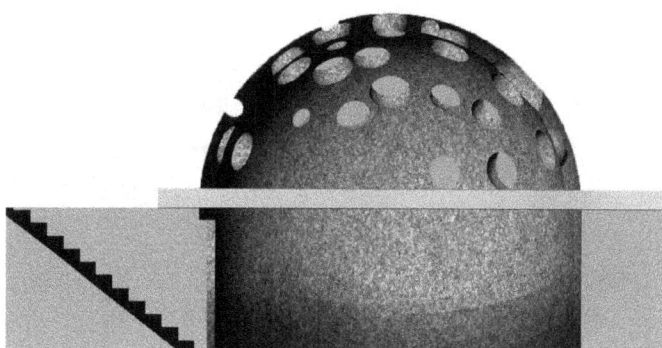

Early Materials and Section

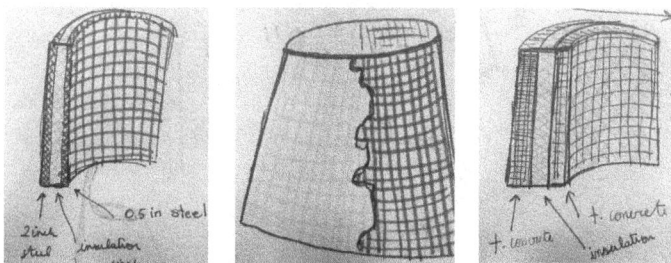

Site Map, Diagrams and Model Renderings

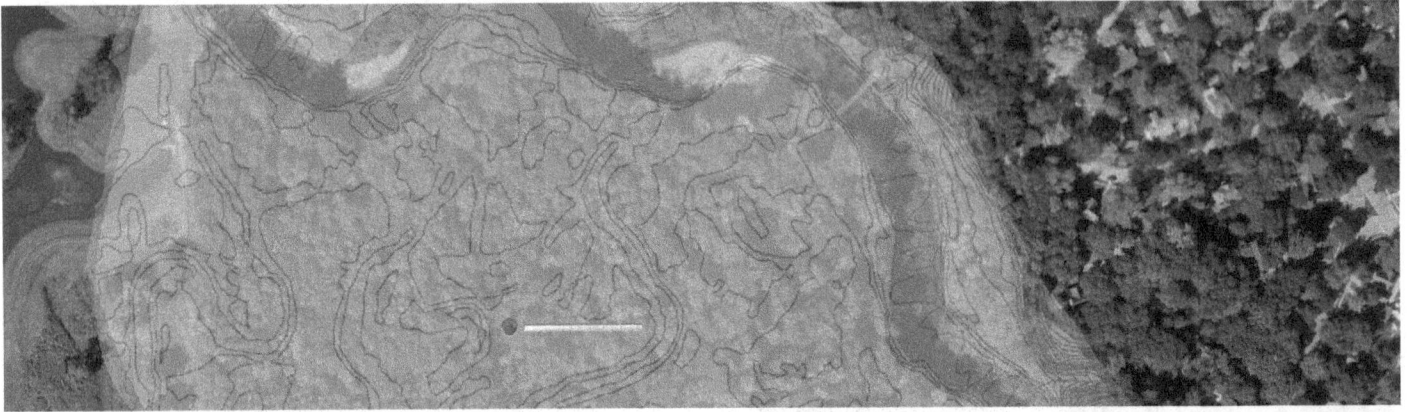

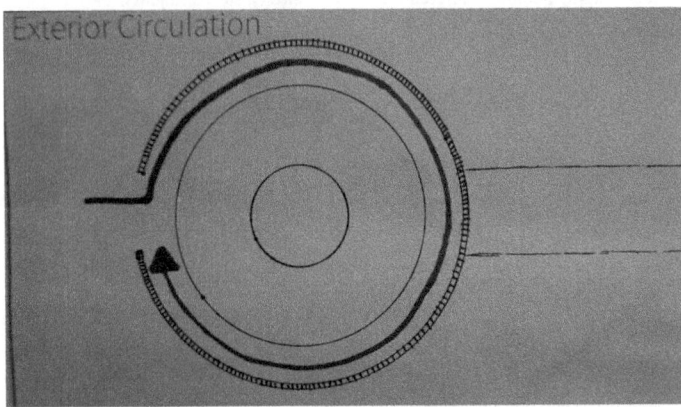

Exterior Circulation

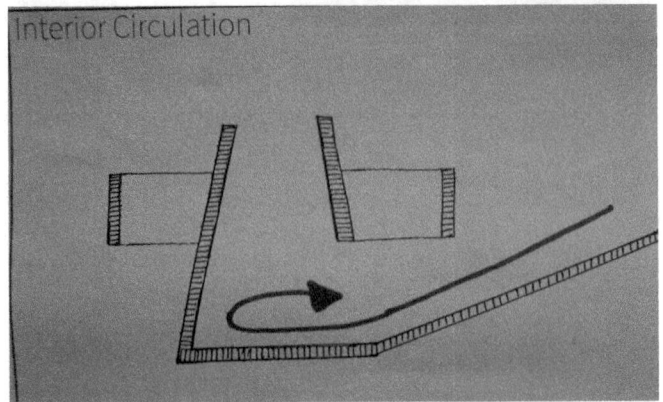

Interior Circulation

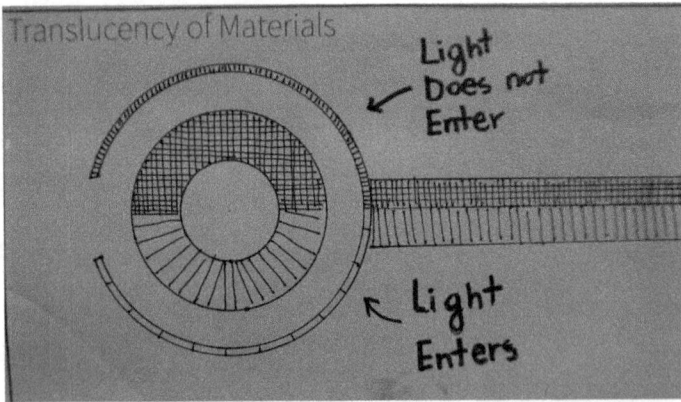

Translucency of Materials

Light Does not Enter

Light Enters

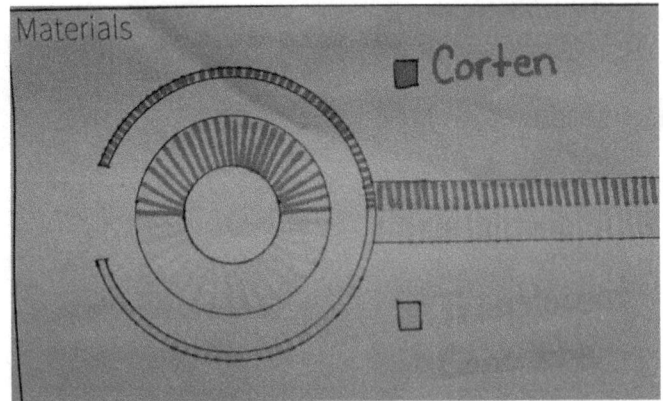

Materials

Corten

Digital and Physical Model

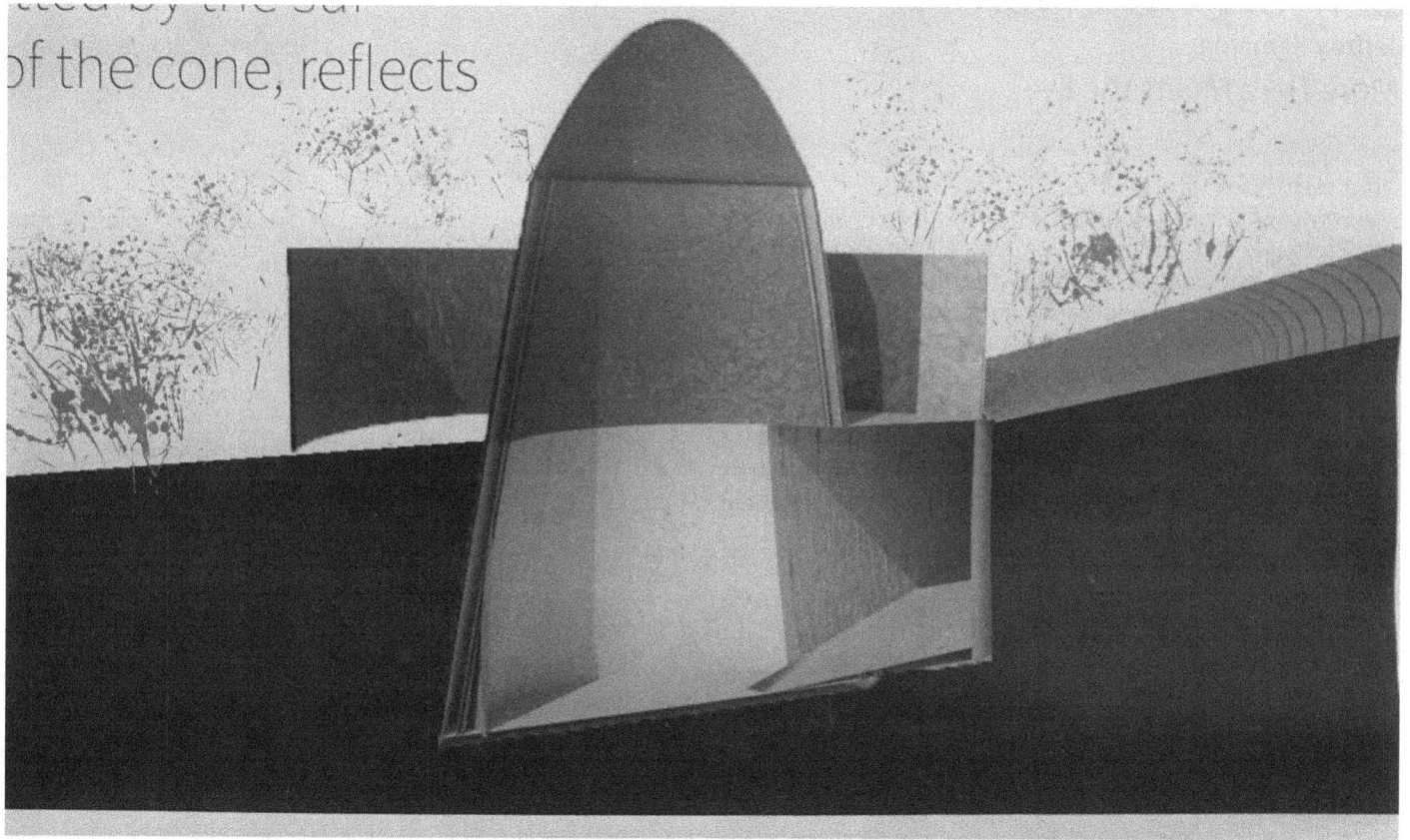

Project 1

Sensory Observatory
Jeffrey Klynsma
More Than Meets the Eye

Site Analysis
The Sensory Observatory project began with an analysis of our site, Brookside Park. Following our research, we were tasked to create representations of the site abstracting evidence of plant life, animal life, and sound based on assigned abstract artist. Abstract painter Helen Frankenthaler pours thinned paint onto large canvases, creating soft, intimate landscapes.

To replicate this "quiet intimacy," I smeared pastel over paper and matboard, as seen in the bottom two images. I then cut the "paintings" into visual sound waves, which represent the parks visual density. Meanwhile, the bold red and soft blue represent the intensity of the sound.

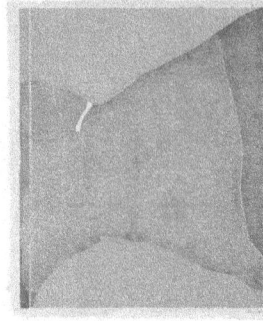

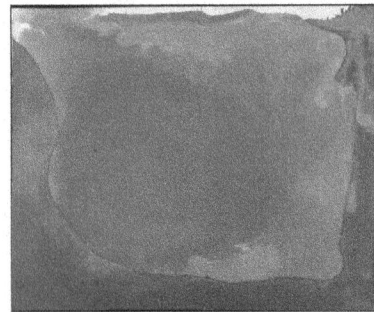

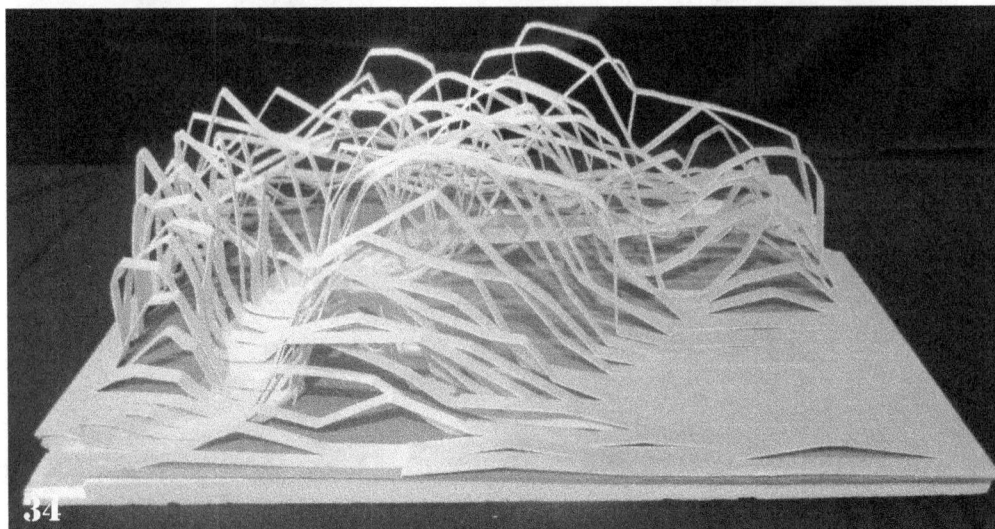

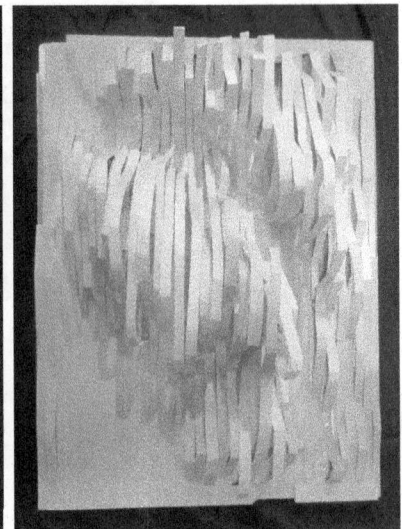

Iteration Process

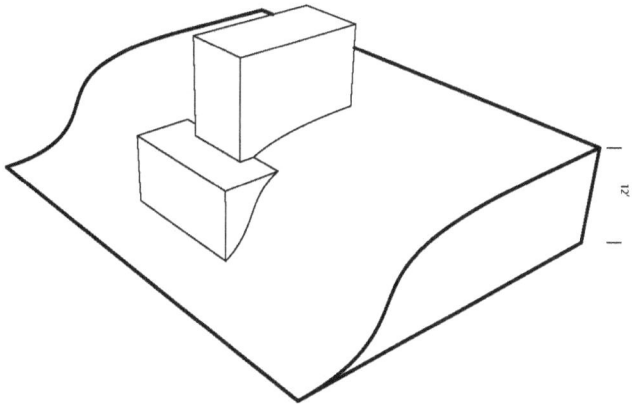
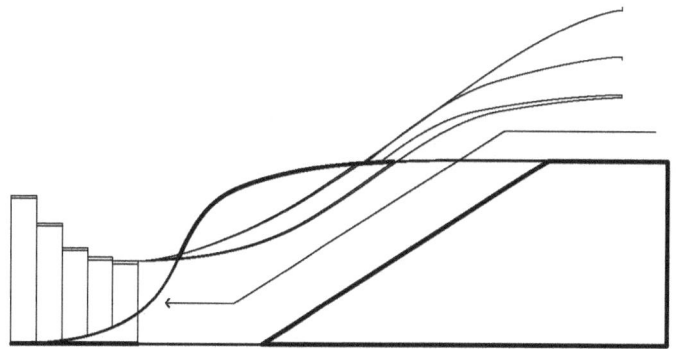

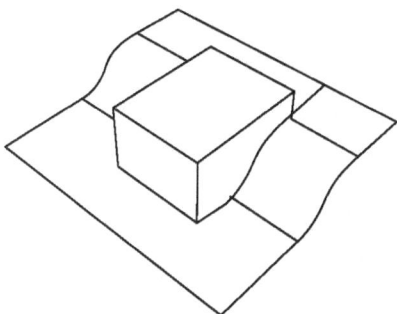
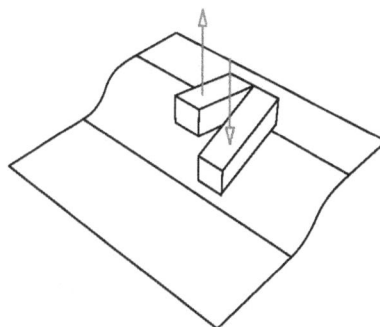
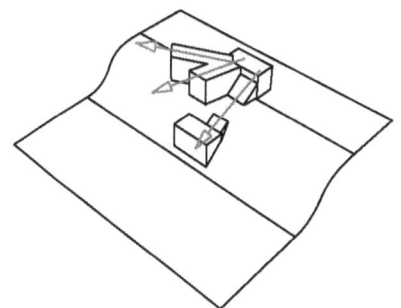

Final Design

"More Than Meets the Eye" seeks to bring the user into various intimate experiences, each wing presenting different parts of the park. The northernmost wing, constructed entirely of wood, brings the user into the trees, screening the view from every direction but up. The central cantilever stretches out over the stream, overlooking the train bridge just a few hundred feet to the south (represented by the black line in the site map to the right). This wing is composed of cor-ten steel, reflecting the rustic materiality of the trains. The southernmost wing stretches down immediately next to the stream. A second stairway brings the user 3.5' beneath water-level, giving the user a more intimate experience with the water. This structure is constructed with a stainless steel frame, which is then filled with glass, replicating the reflective qualities of the water.

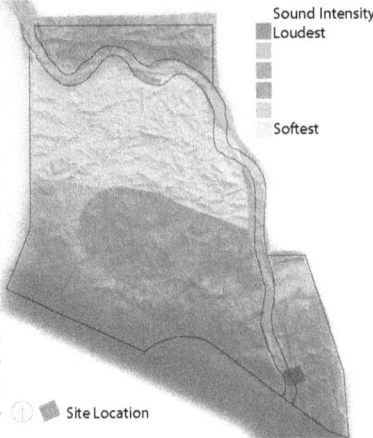

Sound Intensity
Loudest

Softest

Site Location

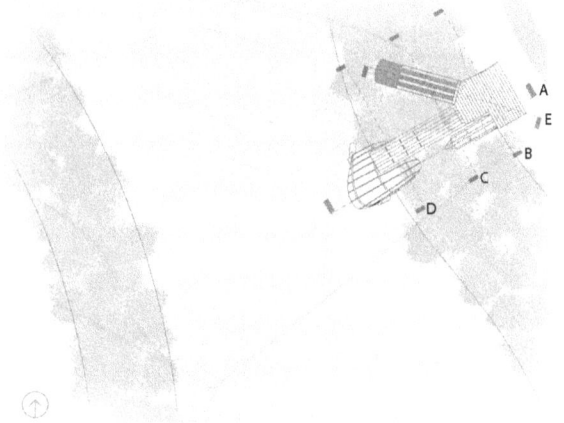

A
E
B
C
D

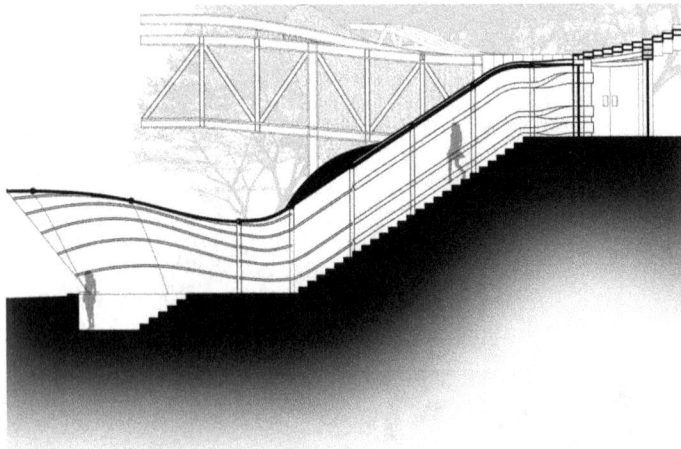

Section A

Structure Diagrams

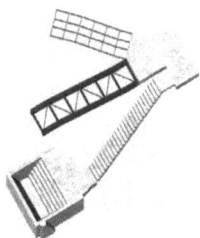

Floor Structure

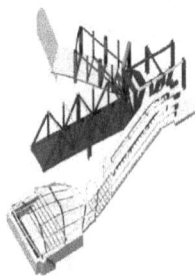

Structural Frame

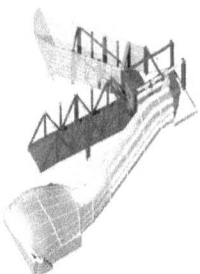

Facade Details

Roof Structure

Section B

Progression Cut 1

Section C

Progression Cut 2

Section D

Progression Cut 3

Section E

Perspective Section

Project 1

Sensory Observatory

Michael McKinney

Limen

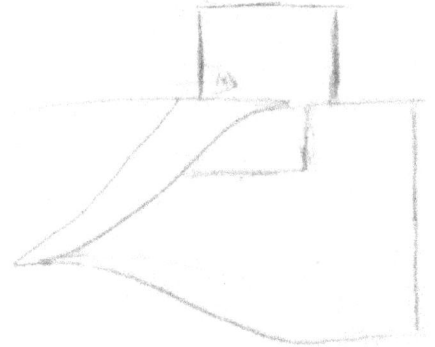

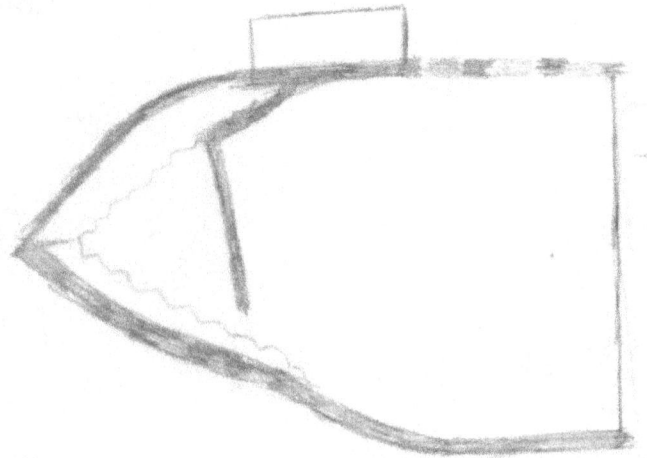

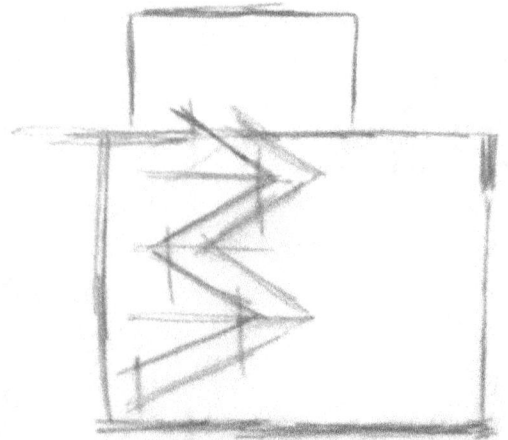

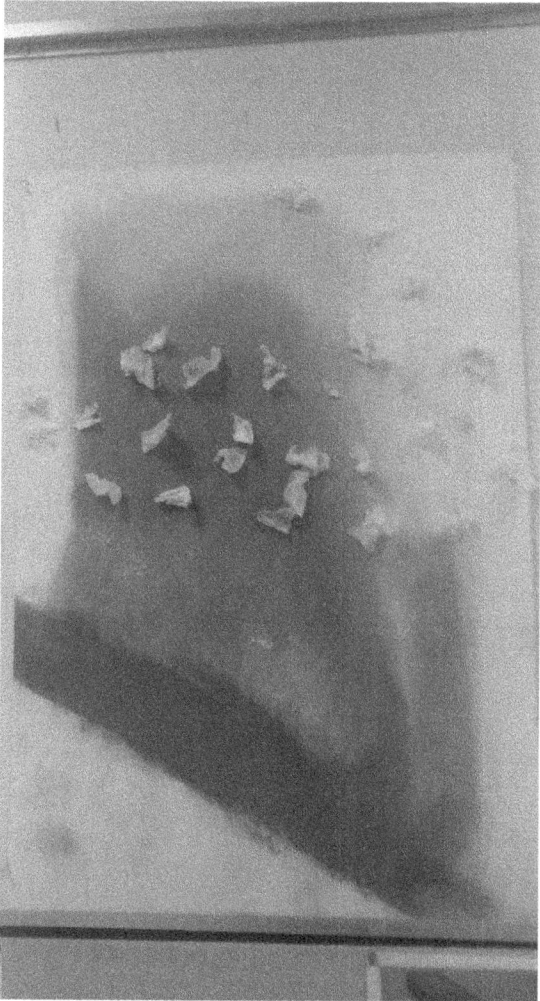

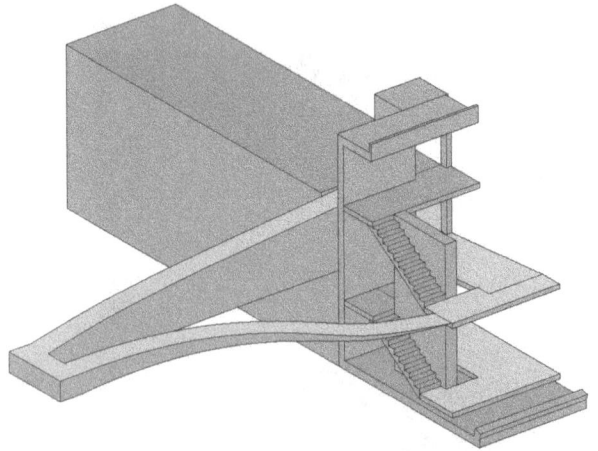

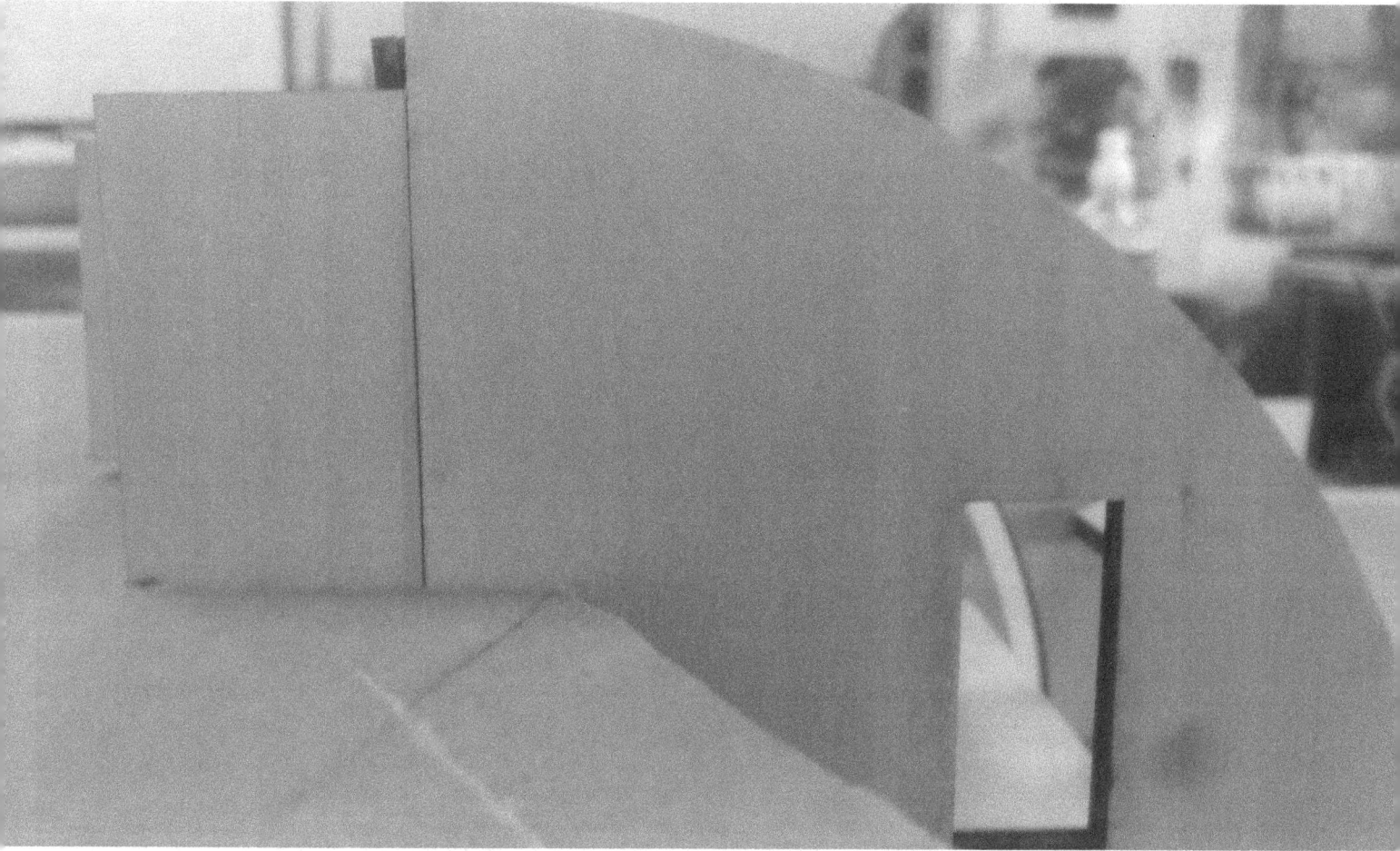

Project 1

Sensory Observatory
Vanessa Miller
Dipper

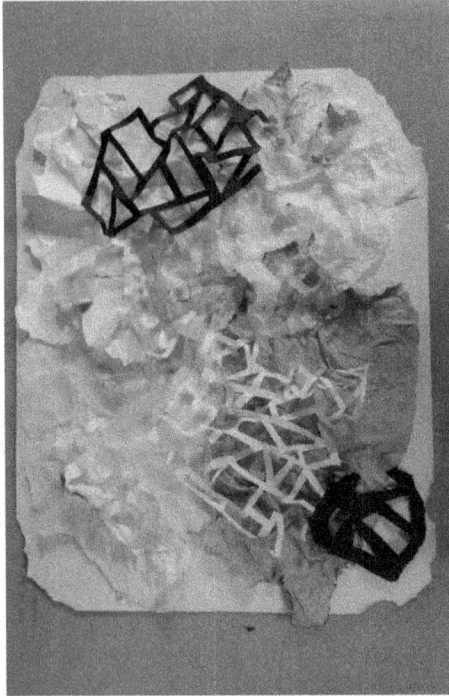

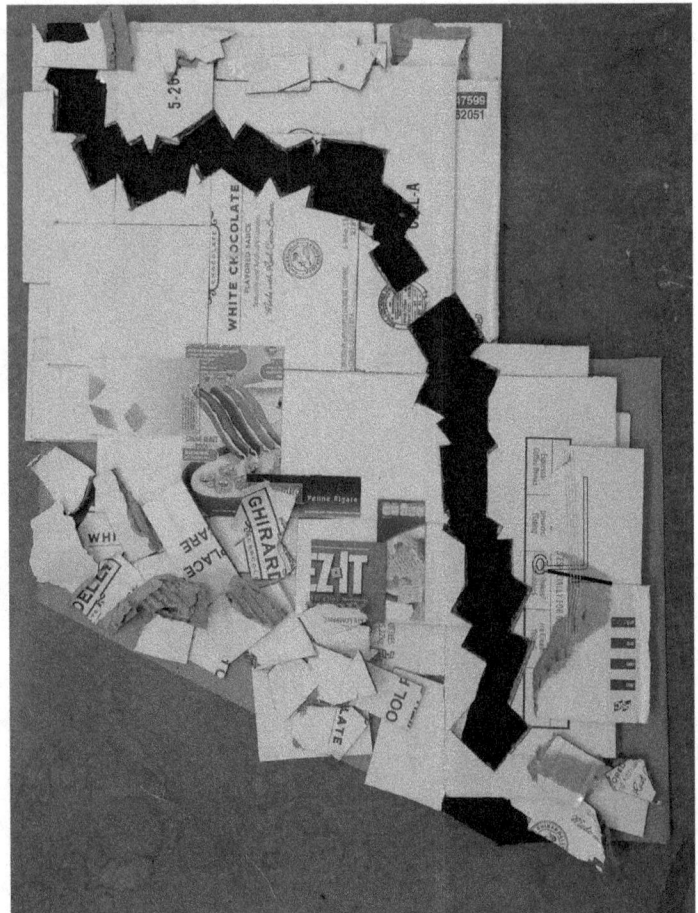

The maps were inspired from the artist Kurt Schwitters, who creates collages of found materials such as newspaper. The rough spaces on the maps represent the parts of the park that are louder or denser, like the space by the train tracks or the parts of the park dense with trees.

My idea for the design is a sky observatory. Compared to many urban places, Iowa skies allow for viewing a great amount of stars. People living in this area, especially children that have lived here all their lives, take for granted all the stars they are able to see. The Dipper is placed strategically overhead of the walk way in Brookside Park to catch the attention of people walking underneath and force people to look up. However when they look up they realize they need to enter the observatory to get a better view of the stars. The oval design of the observatory is inspired from The Roden Crater and the desire for the observatory to feel alien within the park. The viewing space of the observatory has a sloped floor to allow viewers to lean back as they watch the stars or the sky. When in the viewing space a person is focused on the sky by being separated from the Earth. As opposed to standing underneath the observatory where a person is separated from the sky and connected to the Earth and park surroundings.

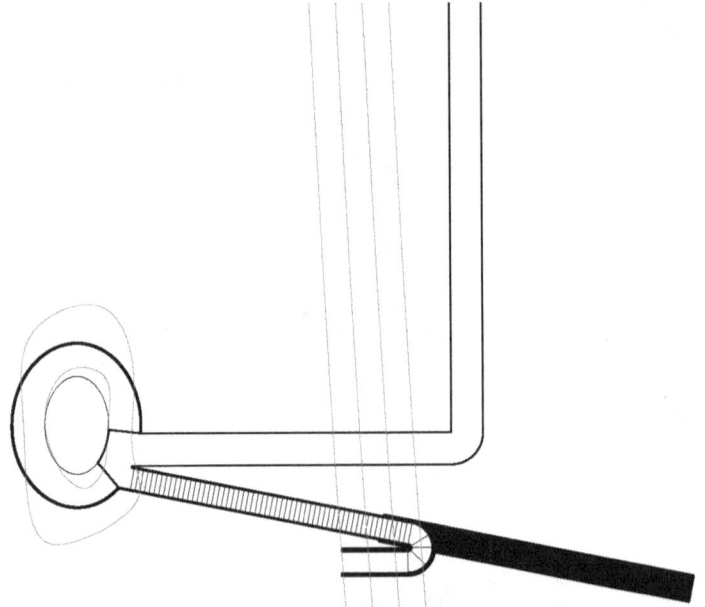

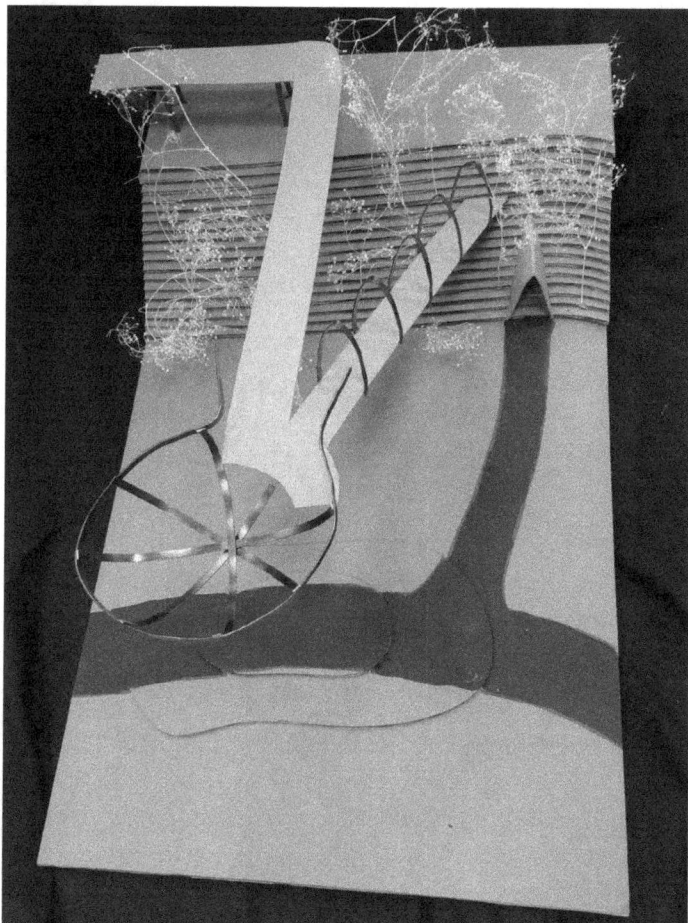
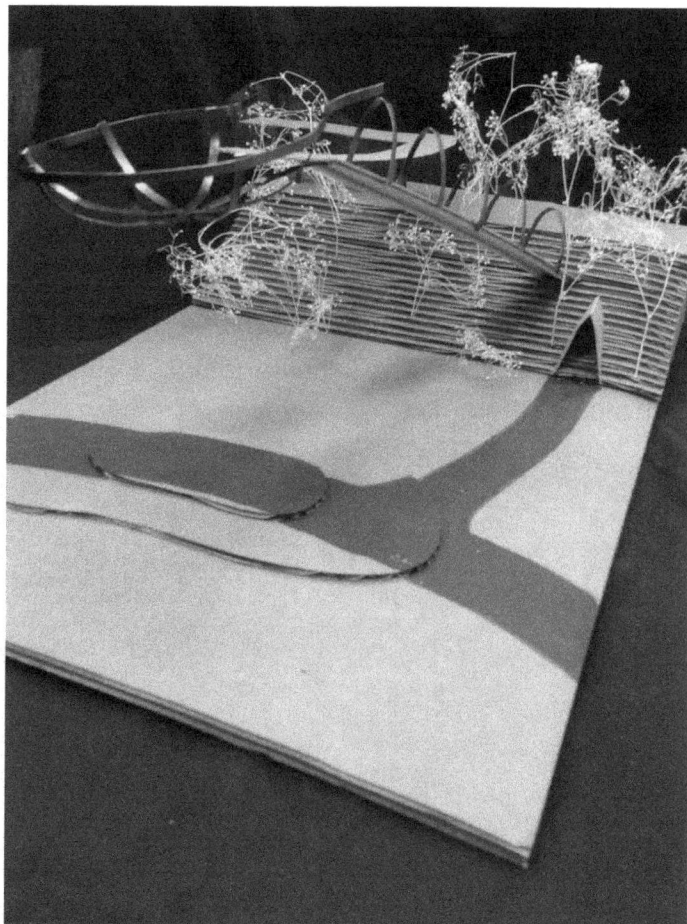

Project 1

Sensory Observatory

Carlos Poémape

Contemplative Observatory

PROCESS

Site analysis and abstraction of Brookside Park in Ames. The models were made taking into consideration the vegetation density and train that passes next to the park and were made using recycled materials. The initial model took Richard Serra as a reference.

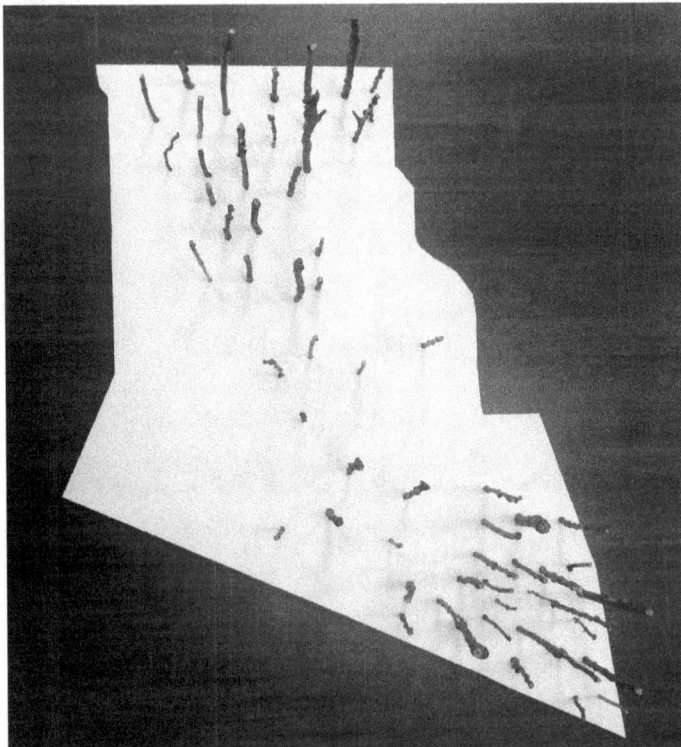

N
500 ft

SECTION

PLAN

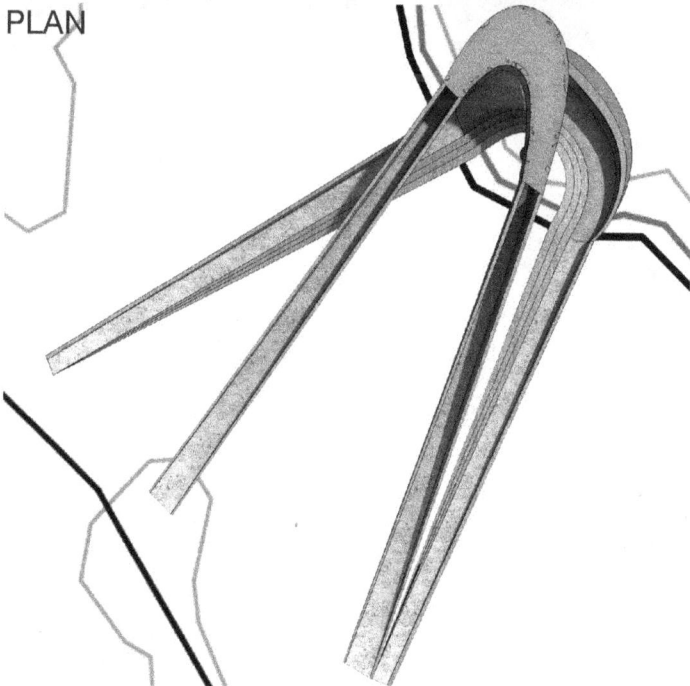

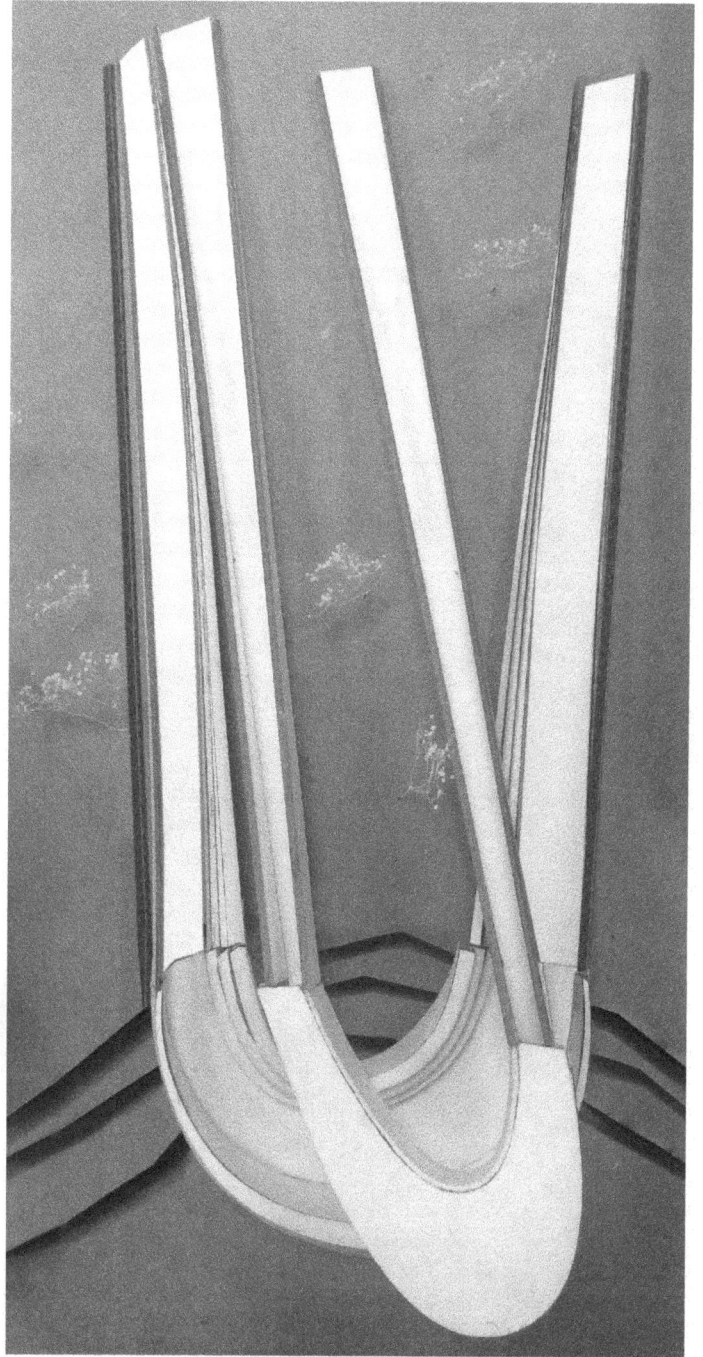

47

APERTURES 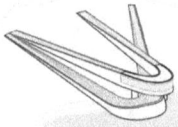 CIRCULATION  CONDITIONED VS UNCONDITIONED 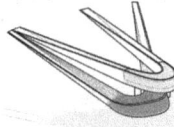 STRUCTURE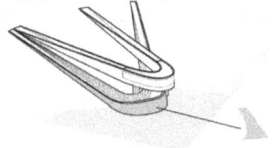

SPATIAL EXPERIENCE SEQUENCE

As visitors walk through Brookside Park in Ames, they see a gravel path that stems out of the main trail. The path leads them to a concrete structure at the edge of Squaw Creek. They have two options:

1. Visitors who follow the wide path at ground level will notice that it gets narrow as they move forward. The walls also get higher. The path wraps visitors as they progress through it. The narrowing path has a bright focal point at its end. The focal point is an inclined indoor space facing north. The platform holding this space is located beyond the creek bank, allowing an uninterrupted view of the sky. Visitors get a wide range of views as they move throughout the convexity of the space and eventually exit.

2. Visitors who follow the narrow path going below ground level will notice that it gets wider as they progress. As they move forward, they reach the creek bank and descend below water level. The wall holding the water varies in height, indicating the water level, which changes depending on the time of the year. The river barely overflows through the wall, creating a cascade. Visitors can sit and contemplate the sky as they enjoy the water sounds in the background.

Project 1

Sensory Observatory

Atalie Ruhnke

Riparian

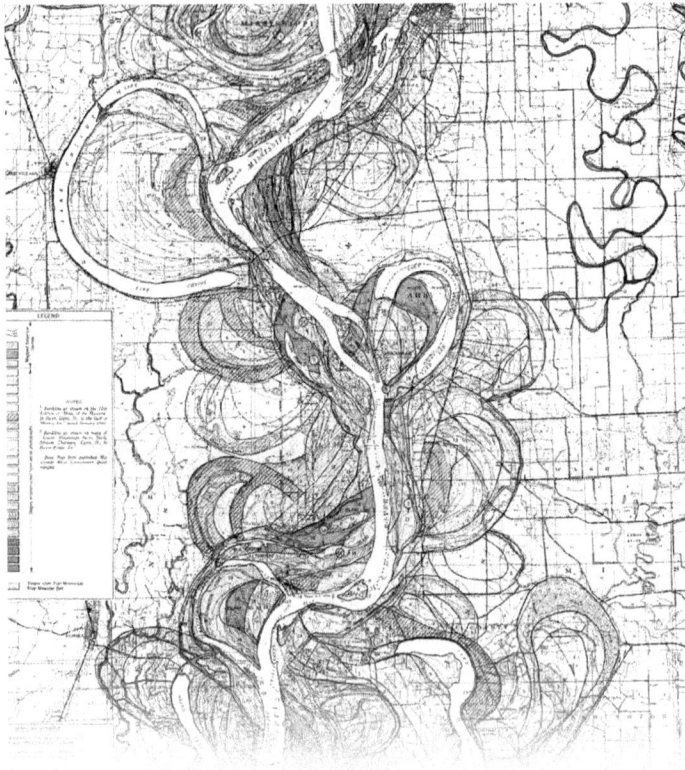

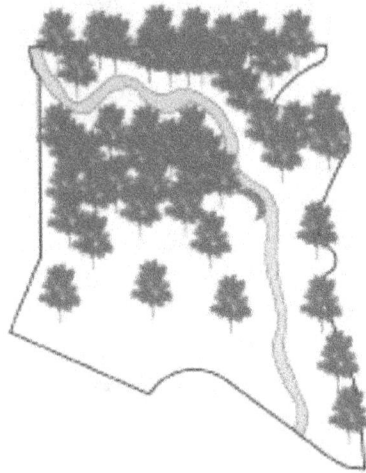

The structure sits in the transitionary part of the site where the the sparse trees become the dense forest.

By re-routing the existing circulation, it allows a larger audience to experience the river and landscape.

The objective of this project was to create an observatory that gave the inhabitants a multi-sensory experience of their surroundings. The subject of the observation was our decision to make, be it the stars, landscape, or any other element of our site. Our site could be located anywhere within Brookside Park in Ames, Iowa. My site was situated on a riverbend with the river becoming the subject of observation. This location provided views upriver and downriver and was situated in a point of transition within the park where the open fields gradually transformed into the dense forest. The structure becomes a continuation of a path through the park, so even those simply passing through could take part in observing the river. The location on the riverbend facilitated interaction between individuals and their natural surroundings, allowing them to truly experience the landscape.

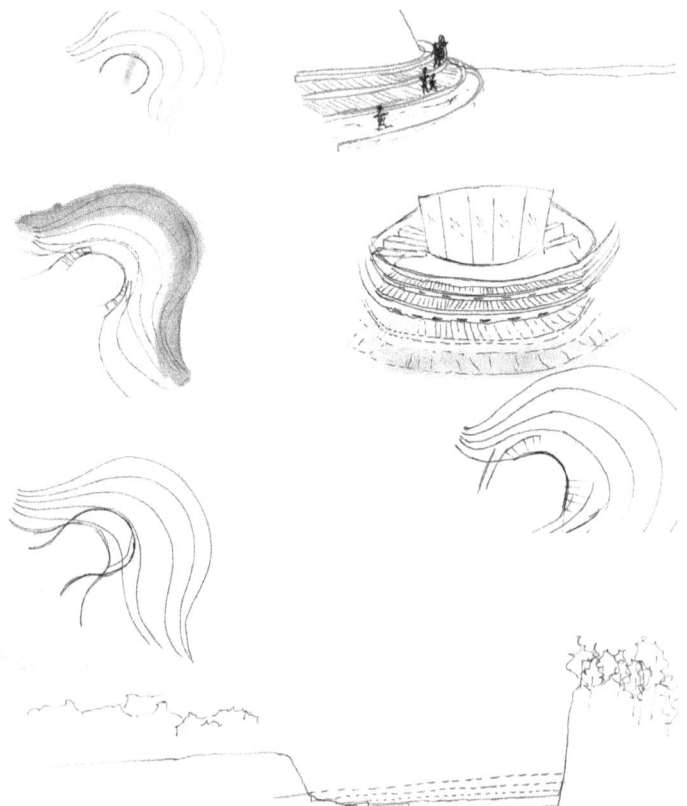

Studying the river and how it changes over time, both the edges of the banks and the water levels inspired the observatory's form.

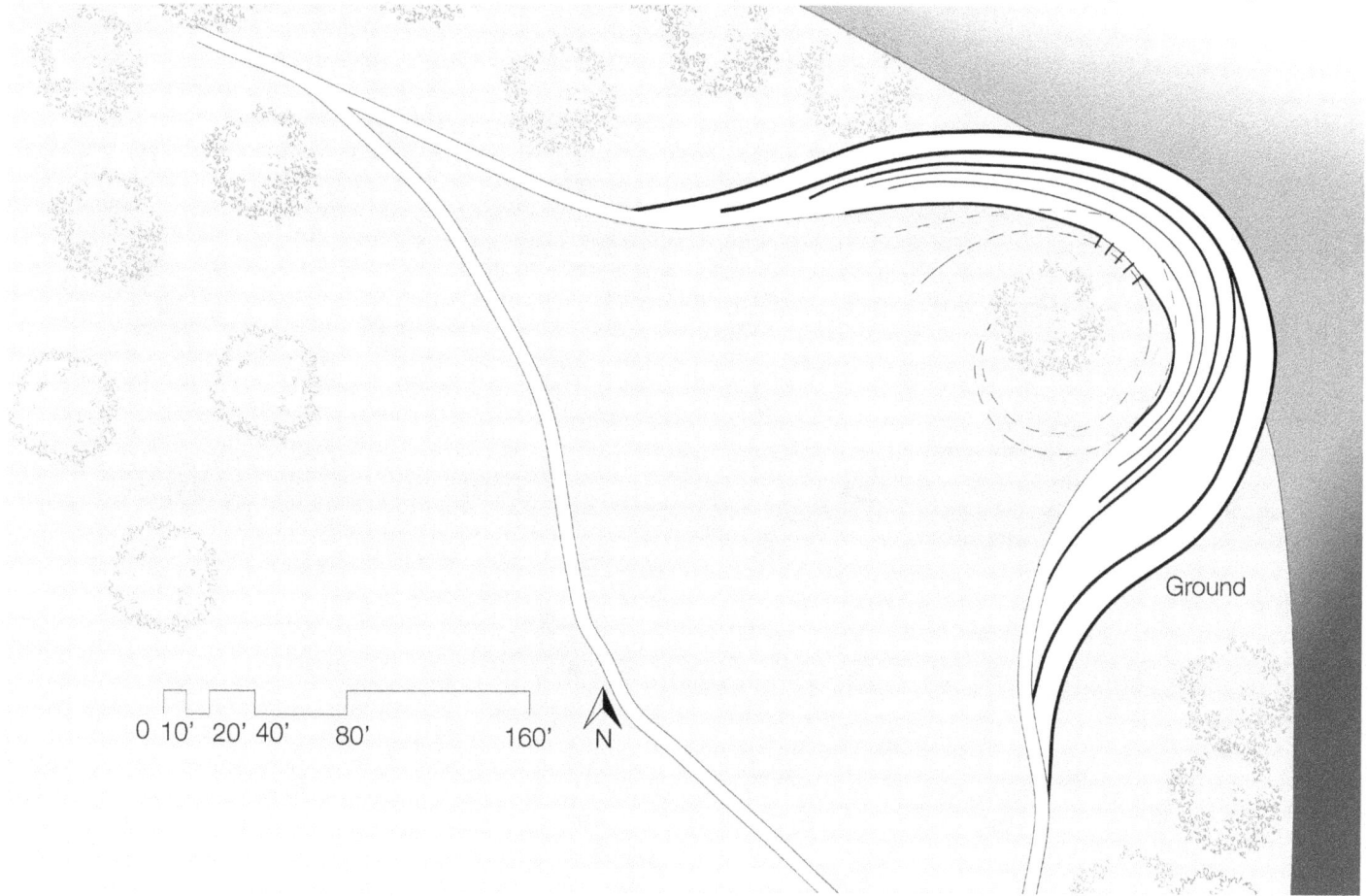

Ground

0 10' 20' 40'   80'   160'   N

In plan, the main circulation path divides into multiple pathways allowing occupants to choose from a variety of experiences.

The structure itself, with its pathways stair-stepping down, becomes the transition between land and water.

Rather than being situated atop a site, the different pathways cut into the earth, literally placing the occupants within the landscape.

51

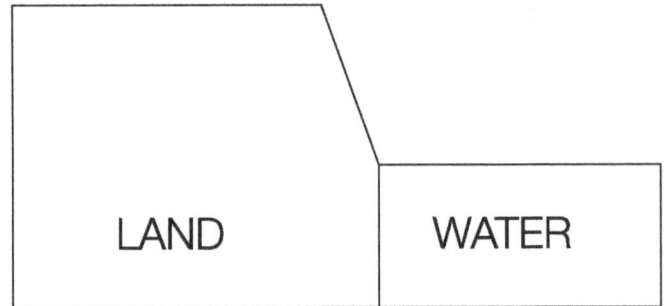

One significant aspect of Riparian was to provide occupants with a variety of sensory experiences. Visitors have a choice and experience the space rather than simply inhabiting it by overlooking the river, viewing it from a protected space, feeling the water haptically, or viewing the river from an unseen perspective, under the water.

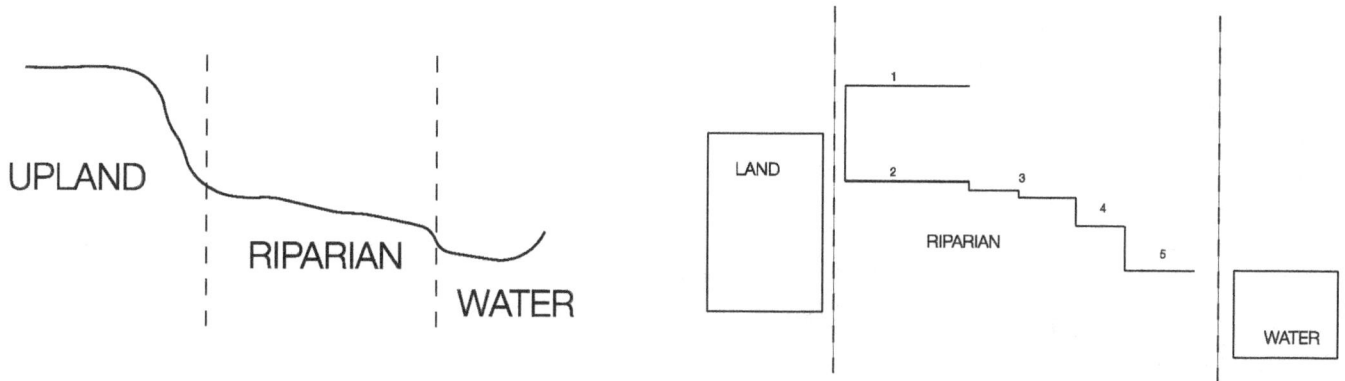

Project 1

Sensory Observatory

Yihuan Zhang

Into Forrest

The site is locate in the brookside park. There are train rail on the south edge of the park. Walk from the south to north, it is like walk into the forrest. The below right picture is the site map of the park and the red mark is the site I choose to build the observatory.

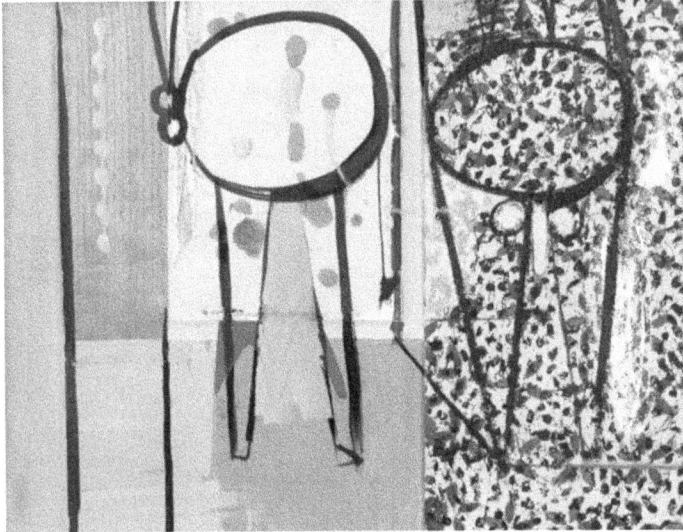

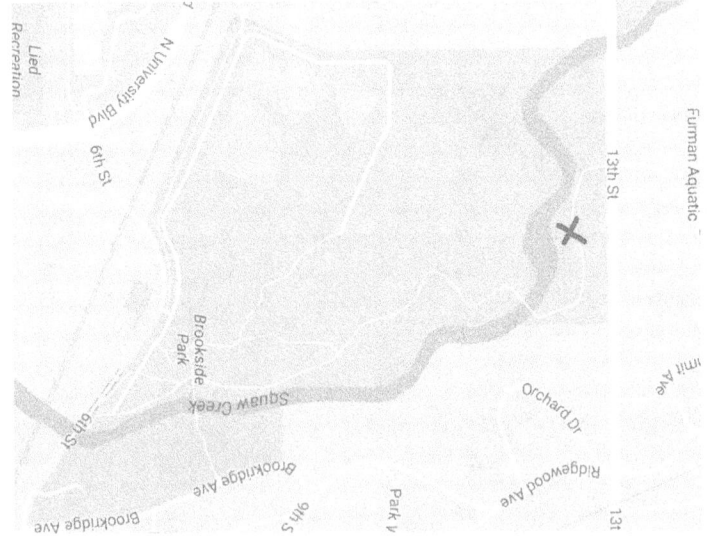

The upper left picture is one of the drawing of my precedent artist.
The first study is site map drawing. I use the twine to represent the path during the trip and the color reprent what I experience during that day.

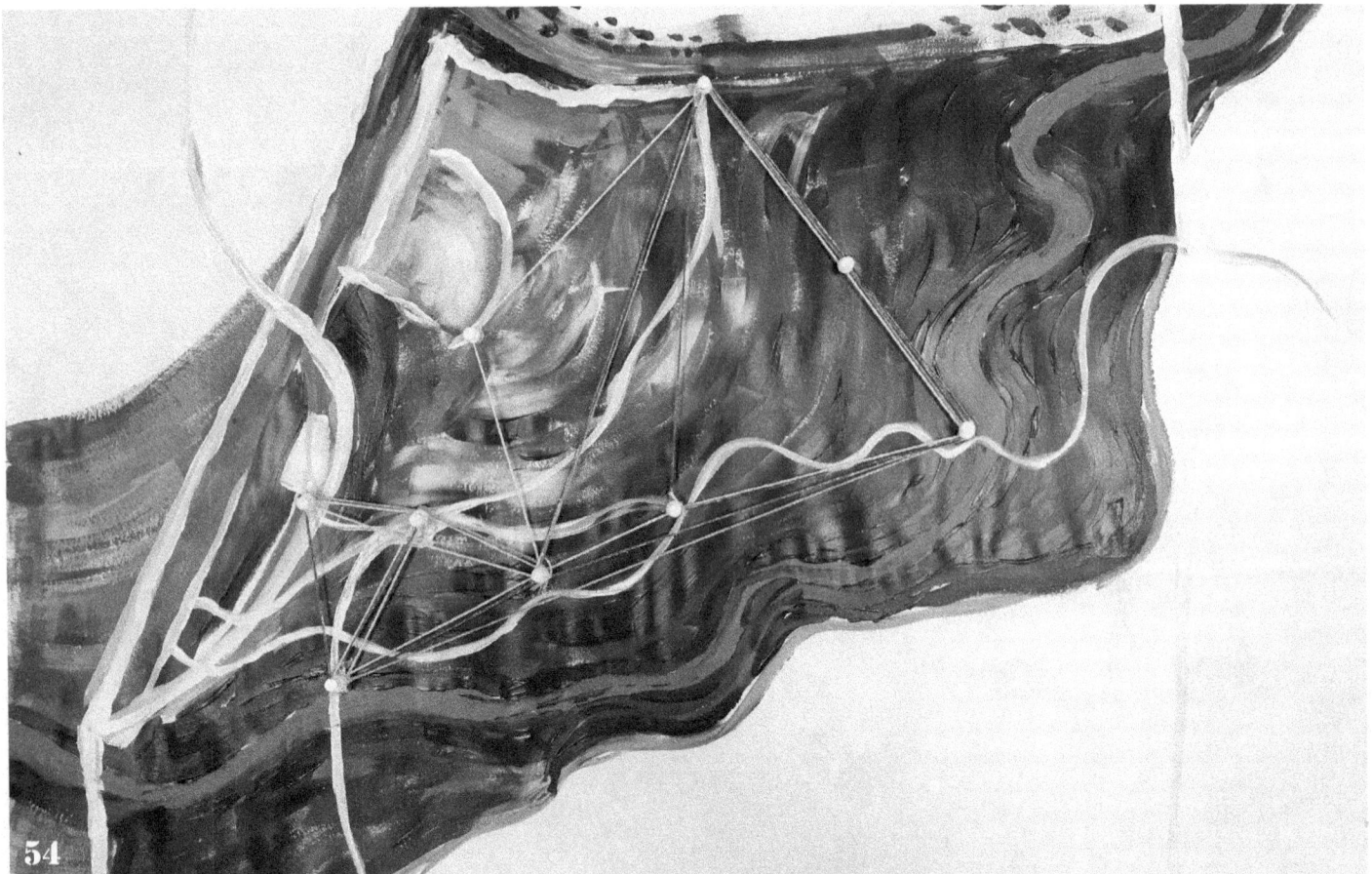

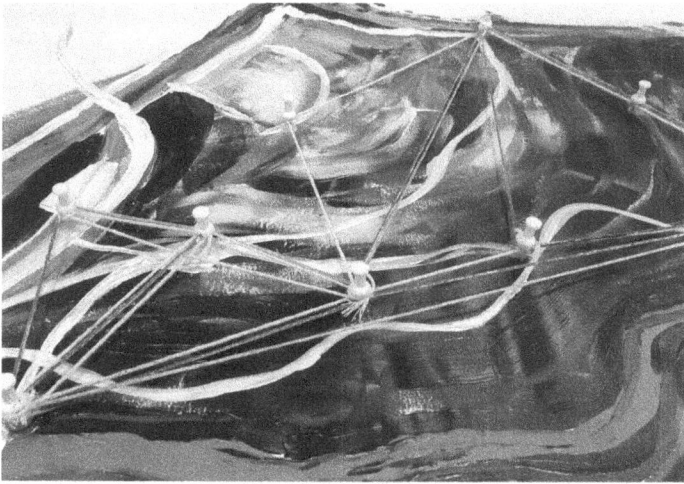

The left up piture is the hybrid drawing of the park, showing the one of the perspective in the park. The piture down below is the abstrct site map model. The red and the nail represent the train on the south of the park. the broken wood stick with the twine represent the river. From the south train rail, we follow the river goes into the park. Deep in the park, there are many trees like a forrest, apart from the civil. The newspaper represent the trees in the park, because the sound of scratching paper like the sound of the wind blowing the leaves. The paper sack like a pile of ash, shows the circle of like, like the leaves falls. The model is from the up to down, shows the feeling of deep into the forrest.

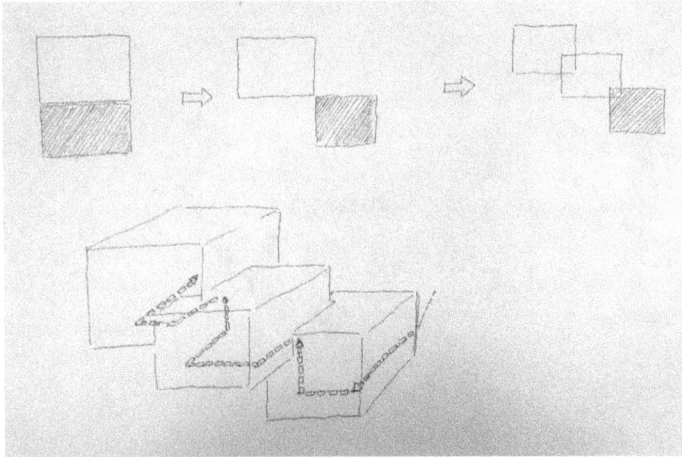

My design for the abservatory is focus on the space feeling in the park, like the feeling when I was walking into the park, into the forrest. The space is getting darker, light goes through between the leaves.

So, I want to make the observatory can give people the opposite feeling, from darker, deeper space to lighter, higher spce. the design has three space from, from the underground to the above gound. The under ground space and the above ground space only have the light goes through the gaps.

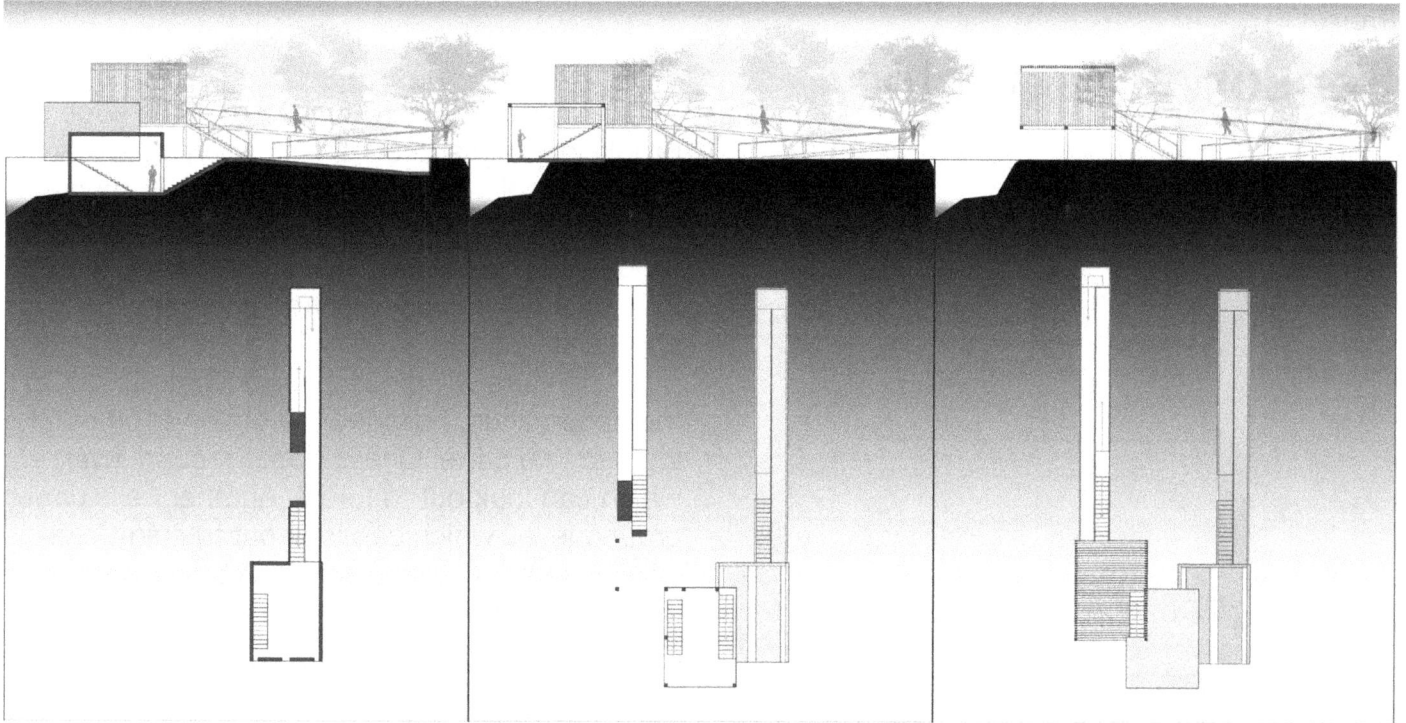

This page shows the plan, section drawing, remdered perspective drawings and model of my design. I use different material to build the three different space, concrete for underground, matel for middle one, and wood for above ground. Each material also gives people the feeling of heavy to light, dark to bright, like the opposite way feeling into the forrest.

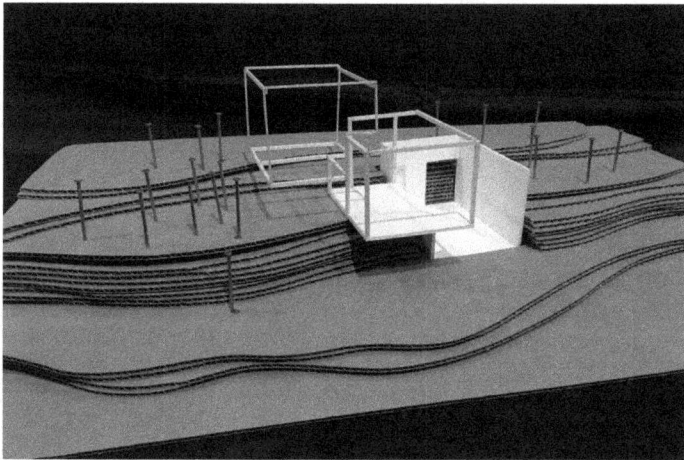

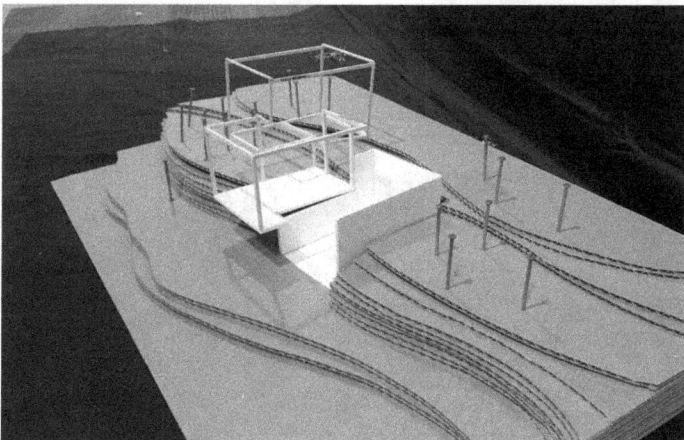

Project 1

Sensory Observatory

Zheng Yang
Box in Wood
Site Plan

Description

My observation is located by the edge of Brookside Park's forest and near the lake. It's about 50 meters away from the main pathway. The mission of my design is to create a space, which can provide two views for visitors, one view is about enjoy forest and another view is to appreciate lake.

Visitors will cross a narrow path to get to the observation. I divided the observation building into two parts. One is upper ground level, which can look out to forest. Another ne is under ground level, which can look out to enjoy lake view. I creat a stressed entrance and a open inside for visitors, which can make visitors feel interesting when experience difference spaces .

In order to match surrounding environment, I choose gary concrete and dark wood as the material and metal hand railling. To get more light in, the observation roof is glass, but other part of the roof is gray concrete.

Hybird Drawing

Diagram

Circulation

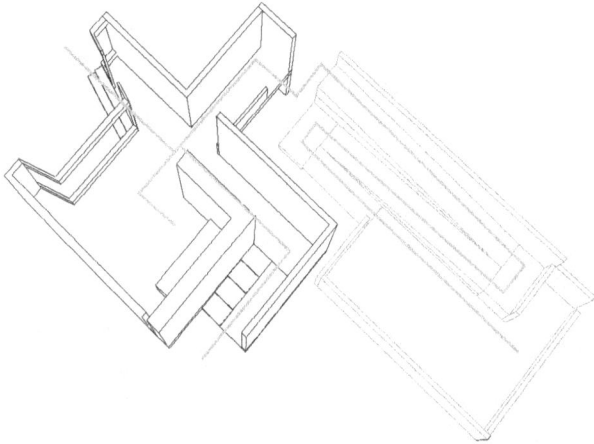

Inside Renderer

Section Cut B-B

Outside Renderer

Section Cut A-A

Final Model

Process Works
Artist Research

Paul Klee

View Towards The Port Of Hammamet

Dream City

Cote De Provence

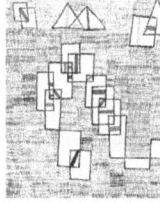

Ad Parnassum

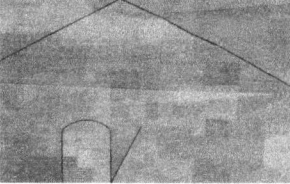

Architecture Of The Plain

Characters In Yellow

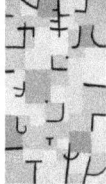

Drawing of site

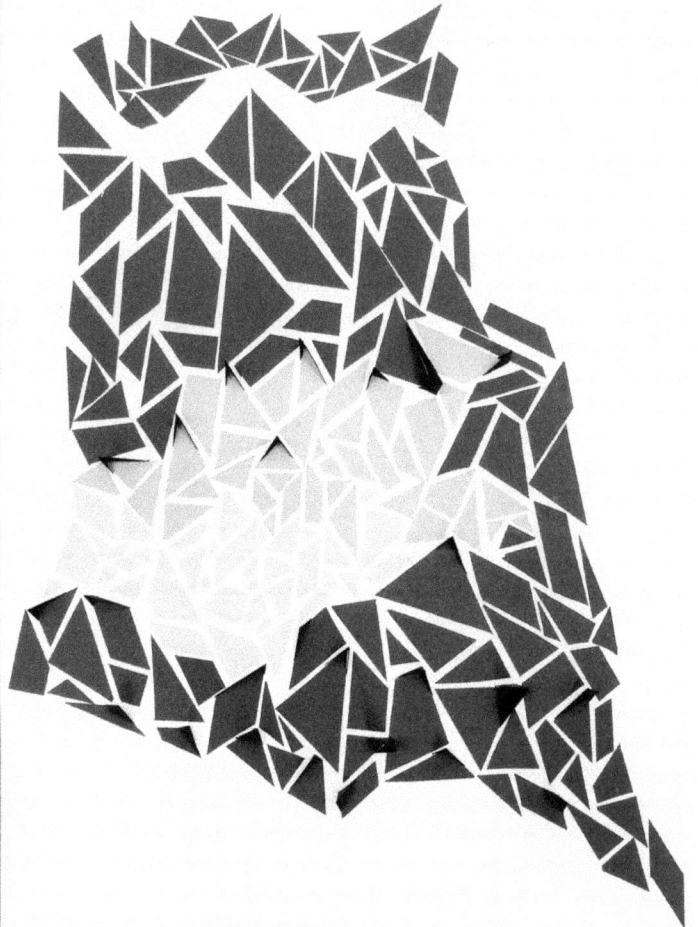

Abstract model of site

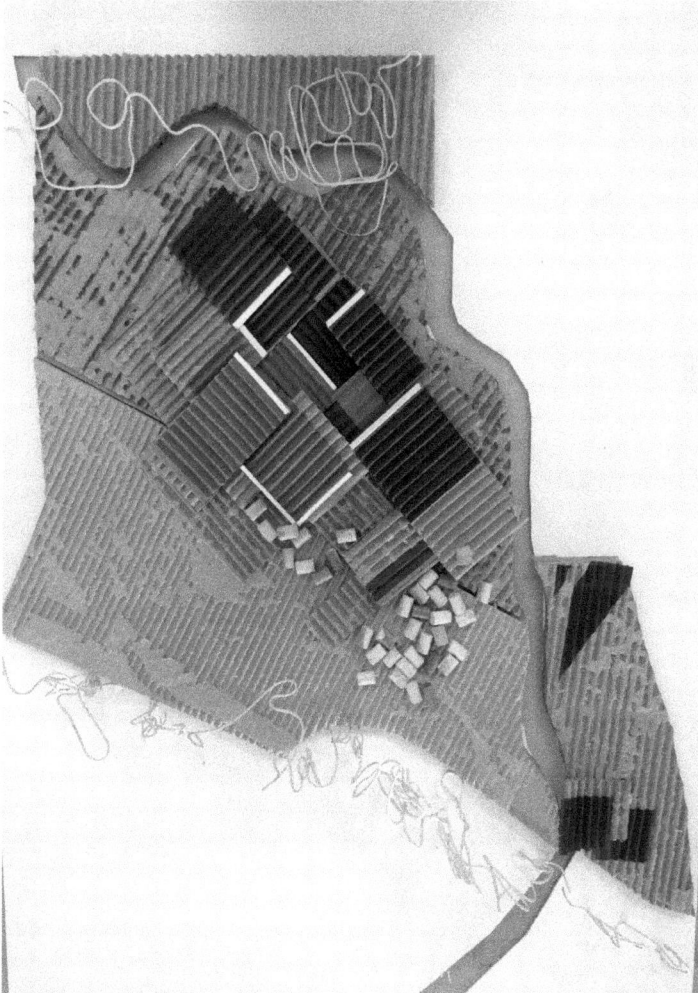

Drawing of site

www.ingramcontent.com/pod-product-compliance
Lightning Source LLC
Chambersburg PA
CBHW081651270326
41933CB00018B/3427